SUBURBAN SKETCHES

W. D. HOWELLS

1st WORLD
LIBRARY
Literary Society

Suburban Sketches

W.D. Howells

© 1st World Library, 2007
PO Box 2211
Fairfield, IA 52556
www.1stworldlibrary.com
First Edition

LCCN: 2007927870

Softcover ISBN: 978-1-4218-4579-1
Hardcover ISBN: 978-1-4218-4495-4
eBook ISBN: 978-1-4218-4663-7

Purchase *"Suburban Sketches"*
as a traditional bound book at:
www.1stWorldLibrary.com/purchase.asp?ISBN=978-1-4218-4579-1

1st World Library is a literary, educational organization
dedicated to:

- Creating a free internet library of downloadable ebooks

- Hosting writing competitions and offering book
publishing scholarships.

Interested in more 1st World Library books?
contact: literacy@1stworldlibrary.com
Check us out at: www.1stworldlibrary.com

1ˢᵗ World Library Literary Society

Giving Back to the World

"If you want to work on the core problem, it's early school literacy."

-James Barksdale, former CEO of Netscape

"No skill is more crucial to the future of a child, or to a democratic and prosperous society, than literacy."

-Los Angeles Times

"Literacy... means far more than learning how to read and write... The aim is to transmit... knowledge and promote social participation."

-UNESCO

"Literacy is not a luxury, it is a right and a responsibility. If our world is to meet the challenges of the twenty-first century we must harness the energy and creativity of all our citizens."

-President Bill Clinton

"Parents should be encouraged to read to their children, and teachers should be equipped with all available techniques for teaching literacy, so the varying needs and capacities of individual kids can be taken into account."

-Hugh Mackay

CONTENTS

MRS. JOHNSON

It was on a morning of the lovely New England May that
we left the horse-car, and, spreading our umbrellas,
walked down the street to our new home in Charlesbridge,
through a storm of snow and rain so finely blent by the
influences of this fortunate climate, that no flake knew
itself from its sister drop, or could be better identified by
the people against whom they beat in unison. A vernal
gale from the east fanned our cheeks and pierced our
marrow and chilled our blood, while the raw, cold green
of the adventurous grass on the borders of the sopping
sidewalks gave, as it peered through its veil of melting
snow and freezing rain, a peculiar cheerfulness to the
landscape. Here and there in the vacant lots abandoned
hoop-skirts defied decay; and near the half-finished
wooden houses, empty mortar-beds, and bits of lath and
slate strewn over the scarred and mutilated ground, added
their interest to the scene. A shaggy drift hung upon the
trees before our own house (which had been built some
years earlier), while its swollen eaves wept silently and
incessantly upon the embankments lifting its base several
feet above the common level.

This heavenly weather, which the Pilgrim Fathers, with
the idea of turning their thoughts effectually from earthly
pleasures, came so far to discover, continued with slight
amelioration throughout the month of May and far into

June; and it was a matter of constant amazement with one who had known less austere climates, to behold how vegetable life struggled with the hostile skies, and, in an atmosphere as chill and damp as that of a cellar, shot forth the buds and blossoms upon the pear-trees, called out the sour Puritan courage of the currant-bushes, taught a reckless native grape-vine to wander and wanton over the southern side of the fence, and decked the banks with violets as fearless and as fragile as New England girls; so that about the end of June, when the heavens relented and the sun blazed out at last, there was little for him to do but to redden and darken the daring fruits that had attained almost their full growth without his countenance.

Then, indeed, Charlesbridge appeared to us a kind of Paradise. The wind blew all day from the southwest, and all day in the grove across the way the orioles sang to their nestlings. The butcher's wagon rattled merrily up to our gate every morning; and if we had kept no other reckoning, we should have known it was Thursday by the grocer. We were living in the country with the conveniences and luxuries of the city about us. The house was almost new and in perfect repair; and, better than all, the kitchen had as yet given no signs of unrest in those volcanic agencies which are constantly at work there, and which, with sudden explosion, make Herculaneums and Pompeiis of so many smiling households. Breakfast, dinner, and tea came up with illusive regularity, and were all the most perfect of their kind; and we laughed and feasted in our vain security. We had out from the city to banquet with us the friends we loved, and we were inexpressibly proud before them of the Help, who first wrought miracles of cookery in our honor, and then appeared in a clean white apron, and the glossiest black hair, to wait upon the table. She was young, and certainly very pretty; she was as gay as a lark, and was courted by a young man whose clothes would have been a credit, if they had not been a reproach, to our lowly basement. She joyfully assented to the idea of staying with us till she married.

In fact, there was much that was extremely pleasant about the little place when the warm weather came, and it was not wonderful to us that Jenny was willing to remain. It was very quiet; we called one another to the window if a large dog went by our door; and whole days passed without the movement of any wheels but the butcher's upon our street, which flourished in ragweed and butter-cups and daisies, and in the autumn burned, like the borders of nearly all the streets in Charlesbridge, with the pallid azure flame of the succory. The neighborhood was in all things a frontier between city and country. The horse-cars, the type of such civilization—full of imposture, discomfort, and sublime possibility—as we yet possess, went by the head of our street, and might, perhaps, be available to one skilled in calculating the movements of comets; while two minutes' walk would take us into a wood so wild and thick that no roof was visible through the trees. We learned, like innocent pastoral people of the golden age, to know the several voices of the cows pastured in the vacant lots, and, like engine-drivers of the iron age, to distinguish the different whistles of the locomotives passing on the neighboring railroad. The trains shook the house as they thundered along, and at night were a kind of company, while by day we had the society of the innumerable birds. Now and then, also, the little ragged boys in charge of the cows—which, tied by long ropes to trees, forever wound themselves tight up against the trunks, and had to be unwound with great ado of hooting and hammering—came and peered lustfully through the gate at our ripening pears. All round us carpenters were at work building new houses; but so far from troubling us, the strokes of their hammers fell softly upon the sense, like one's heart-beats upon one's own consciousness in the lapse from all fear of pain under the blessed charm of an anaesthetic.

We played a little at gardening, of course, and planted tomatoes, which the chickens seemed to like, for they ate them up as fast as they ripened; and we watched with pride the growth of our Lawton blackberries, which, after attaining the most stalwart proportions, were still as bitter as the scrubbiest of their savage brethren, and which, when by advice left on the vines for a week after they turned black, were silently gorged by secret and gluttonous flocks of robins and orioles. As for our grapes, the frost cut them off in the hour of their triumph.

So, as I have hinted, we were not surprised that Jenny should be willing to remain with us, and were as little prepared for her desertion as for any other change of our moral state. But one day in September she came to her nominal mistress with tears in her beautiful eyes and protestations of unexampled devotion upon her tongue, and said that she was afraid she must leave us. She liked the place, and she never had worked for any one that was more of a lady, but she had made up her mind to go into the city. All this, so far, was quite in the manner of domestics who, in ghost stories, give warning to the occupants of haunted houses; and Jenny's mistress listened in suspense for the motive of her desertion, expecting to hear no less than that it was something which walked up and down the stairs and dragged iron links after it, or something that came and groaned at the front door, like populace dissatisfied with a political candidate. But it was in fact nothing of this kind; simply, there were no lamps upon our street, and Jenny, after spending Sunday evening with friends in East Charlesbridge, was always alarmed, on her return, in walking from the horse-car to our door. The case was hopeless, and Jenny and our household parted with respect and regret.

We had not before this thought it a grave disadvantage that our street was unlighted. Our street was not drained nor graded; no municipal cart ever came to carry away our ashes; there was not a water-butt within half a mile to save us from fire, nor more than the one thousandth part of a policeman to protect us from theft. Yet, as I paid a heavy tax, I somehow felt that we enjoyed the benefits of city government, and never looked upon Charlesbridge as in any way undesirable for residence. But when it became necessary to find help in Jenny's place, the frosty welcome given to application at the intelligence offices renewed a painful doubt awakened by her departure. To be sure, the heads of the offices were polite enough; but when the young housekeeper had stated her case at the first to which she applied, and the Intelligencer had called out to the invisible expectants in the adjoining room, "Anny wan wants to do giner'l housewark in Charlsbrudge?" there came from the maids invoked so loud, so fierce, so full a "No!" as shook the lady's heart with an indescribable shame and dread. The name that, with an innocent pride in its literary and historical associations, she had written at the heads of her letters, was suddenly become a matter of reproach to her; and she was almost tempted to conceal thereafter that she lived in Charlesbridge, and to pretend that she dwelt upon some wretched little street in Boston. "You see," said the head of the office, "the gairls doesn't like to live so far away from the city. Now if it was on'y in the Port...."

This pen is not graphic enough to give the remote reader an idea of the affront offered to an inhabitant of Old Charlesbridge in these closing words. Neither am I of sufficiently tragic mood to report here all the sufferings undergone by an unhappy family in finding servants, or to tell how the winter was passed with miserable makeshifts. Alas! is it not the history of a thousand experiences? Any one who looks upon this page could match it with a tale as full of heartbreak and disaster, while I conceive that, in hastening to speak of Mrs. Johnson, I approach a subject of unique interest.

The winter that ensued after Jenny's departure was the true sister of the bitter and shrewish spring of the same year. But indeed it is always with a secret shiver that one must think of winter in our regrettable climate. It is a terrible potency, robbing us of half our lives, and threatening or desolating the moiety left us with rheumatisms and catarrhs. There is a much vaster sum of enjoyment possible to man in the more generous latitudes; and I have sometimes doubted whether even the energy characteristic of ours is altogether to be praised, seeing that it has its spring not so much in pure aspiration as in the instinct of self-preservation. Egyptian, Greek, Roman energy was an inner impulse; but ours is too often the sting of cold, the spur of famine. We must endure our winter, but let us not be guilty of the hypocrisy of pretending that we like it. Let us caress it with no more vain compliments, but use it with something of its own rude and savage sincerity.

I say, our last Irish girl went with the last snow, and on one of those midsummer-like days that sometimes fall in early April to our yet bleak and desolate zone, our hearts sang of Africa and golden joys. A Libyan longing took us, and we would have chosen, if we could, to bear a strand of grotesque beads, or a handful of brazen gauds, and traffic them for some sable maid with crisped locks, whom, uncoffling from the captive train beside the desert, we should make to do our general housework forever, through the right of lawful purchase. But we knew that this was impossible, and that, if we desired colored help, we must seek it at the intelligence office, which is in one of those streets chiefly inhabited by the orphaned children and grandchildren of slavery. To tell the truth these orphans do not seem to grieve much for their bereavement, but lead a life of joyous and rather indolent oblivion in their quarter of the city. They are often to be seen sauntering up and down the street by which the Charlesbridge cars arrive,—the young with a harmless swagger, and the old with the generic limp which our Autocrat has already noted as attending advanced years in their race. They seem the natural human interest of a street so largely devoted to old clothes; and the thoughtful may see a felicity in their presence where the pawn-brokers' windows display the forfeited pledges of improvidence, and subtly remind us that we have yet to redeem a whole race, pawned in our needy and reckless national youth, and still held against us by the Uncle of Injustice, who is also the Father of Lies. How gayly are the young ladies of this race attired, as they trip up and down the side walks, and in and out through the pendent garments at the shop doors! They are the black pansies and marigolds and dark-blooded dahlias among woman-kind. They try to assume something of our colder race's demeanor, but even the passer on the horse-car can see that it is not native with them, and is better pleased when they forget us, and ungenteelly laugh in encountering friends, letting their white teeth glitter through the generous lips that open to their ears. In the streets branching upwards from this avenue, very little colored men and maids play with broken or enfeebled toys, or sport on the wooden pavements of the entrances to the inner courts. Now and then a colored soldier or sailor— looking strange in his uniform, even after the custom of several years—emerges from those passages; or, more rarely, a black gentleman, stricken in years, and cased in shining broadcloth, walks solidly down the brick side-walk, cane in hand,—a vision of serene self-complacency, and so plainly the expression of virtuous public sentiment that the great colored louts, innocent enough till then in their idleness, are taken with a sudden sense of depravity, and loaf guiltily up against the house-walls. At the same moment, perhaps, a young damsel, amorously scuffling with an admirer through one of the low open windows, suspends the strife, and bids him, "Go along now, do!" More rarely yet than the gentleman described, one may see a white girl among the dark neighbors, whose frowzy head is uncovered, and whose sleeves are rolled up to her elbows, and who, though no doubt quite at home, looks as strange there as that pale anomaly which may sometimes be seen among a crew of blackbirds.

An air not so much of decay as of unthrift, and yet hardly of unthrift, seems to prevail in the neighborhood, which has none of the aggressive and impudent squalor of an Irish quarter, and none of the surly wickedness of a low American street. A gayety not born of the things that bring its serious joy to the true New England heart—a ragged gayety, which comes of summer in the blood, and not in the pocket or the conscience, and which affects the countenance and the whole demeanor, setting the feet to some inward music, and at times bursting into a line of song or a child-like and irresponsible laugh—gives tone to the visible life, and wakens a very friendly spirit in the passer, who somehow thinks there of a milder climate, and is half persuaded that the orange-peel on the sidewalks came from fruit grown in the soft atmosphere of those back courts.

It was in this quarter, then, that we heard of Mrs. Johnson; and it was from a colored boarding-house there that she came out to Charlesbridge to look at us, bringing her daughter of twelve years with her. She was a matron of mature age and portly figure, with a complexion like coffee soothed with the richest cream; and her manners were so full of a certain tranquillity and grace, that she charmed away all out will to ask for references. It was only her barbaric laughter and her lawless eye that betrayed how slightly her New England birth and breeding covered her ancestral traits, and bridged the gulf of a thousand years of civilization that lay between her race and ours. But in fact, she was doubly estranged by descent; for, as we learned later, a sylvan wildness mixed with that of the desert in her veins: her grandfather was an Indian, and her ancestors on this side had probably sold their lands for the same value in trinkets that bought the original African pair on the other side.

The first day that Mrs. Johnson descended into our kitchen, she conjured from the malicious disorder in which it had been left by the flitting Irish kobold a dinner that revealed the inspirations of genius, and was quite different from a dinner of mere routine and laborious talent. Something original and authentic mingled with the accustomed flavors; and, though vague reminiscences of canal-boat travel and woodland camps arose from the relish of certain of the dishes, there was yet the assurance of such power in the preparation of the whole, that we knew her to be merely running over the chords of our appetite with preliminary savors, as a musician acquaints his touch with the keys of an unfamiliar piano before breaking into brilliant and triumphant execution. Within a week she had mastered her instrument; and thereafter there was no faltering in her performances, which she varied constantly, through inspiration or from suggestion. She was so quick to receive new ideas in her art, that, when the Roman statuary who stayed a few weeks with us explained the mystery of various purely Latin dishes, she caught their principle at once; and visions of the great white cathedral, the Coliseum, and the "dome of Brunelleschi" floated before us in the exhalations of the Milanese *risotto*, Roman *stufadino*, and Florentine *stracotto* that smoked upon our board. But, after all, it was in puddings that Mrs. Johnson chiefly excelled. She was one of those cooks—rare as men of genius in literature—who love their own dishes; and she had, in her personally child-like simplicity of taste, and the inherited appetites of her savage forefathers, a dominant passion for sweets. So far as we could learn, she subsisted principally upon puddings and tea. Through the same primitive instincts, no doubt, she loved praise. She openly exulted in our artless flatteries of her skill; she waited jealously at the head of the kitchen stairs to hear what was said of her work, especially if there were guests; and she was never too weary to attempt emprises of cookery.

While engaged in these, she wore a species of sightly handkerchief like a turban upon her head and about her person those mystical swathings in which old ladies of the African race delight. But she most pleasured our sense of beauty and moral fitness when, after the last pan was washed and the last pot was scraped, she lighted a potent pipe, and, taking her stand at the kitchen door, laded the soft evening air with its pungent odors. If we surprised her at these supreme moments, she took the pipe from her lips, and put it behind her, with a low mellow chuckle, and a look of half-defiant consciousness; never guessing that none of her merits took us half so much as the cheerful vice which she only feigned to conceal.

Some things she could not do so perfectly as cooking, because of her failing eyesight; and we persuaded her that spectacles would both become and befriend a lady of her years, and so bought her a pair of steel-bowed glasses. She wore them in some great emergencies at first, but had clearly no pride in them. Before long she laid them aside altogether, and they had passed from our thoughts, when one day we heard her mellow note of laughter and her daughter's harsher cackle outside our door, and, opening it, beheld Mrs. Johnson in gold-bowed spectacles of massive frame. We then learned that their purchase was in fulfillment of a vow made long ago, in the life-time of Mr. Johnson, that, if ever she wore glasses, they should be

W. D. Howells

gold-bowed; and I hope the manes of the dead were half as happy in these votive spectacles as the simple soul that offered them.

She and her late partner were the parents of eleven children, some of whom were dead, and some of whom were wanderers in unknown parts. During his life-time she had kept a little shop in her native town; and it was only within a few years that she had gone into service. She cherished a natural haughtiness of spirit, and resented control, although disposed to do all she could of her own motion. Being told to say when she wanted an afternoon, she explained that when she wanted an afternoon she always took it without asking, but always planned so as not to discommode the ladies with whom she lived. These, she said, had numbered twenty-seven within three years, which made us doubt the success of her system in all cases, though she merely held out the fact as an assurance of her faith in the future, and a proof of the ease with which places were to be found. She contended, moreover, that a lady who had for thirty years had a house of her own, was in nowise bound to ask permission to receive visits from friends where she might be living, but that they ought freely to come and go like other guests. In this spirit she once invited her son-in-law, Professor Jones of Providence, to dine with her; and her defied mistress, on entering the dining-room, found the Professor at pudding and tea there,—an impressively respectable figure in black clothes, with a black face rendered yet more effective by a pair of green goggles. It appeared that this dark professor was a light of phrenology in Rhode Island, and that he was believed to have uncommon virtue in his science by reason of being blind as well as black.

I am loath to confess that Mrs. Johnson had not a flattering opinion of the Caucasian race in all respects. In fact, she had very good philosophical and Scriptural reasons for looking upon us as an upstart people of new blood, who had come into their whiteness by no creditable or pleasant process. The late Mr. Johnson, who had died in the West Indies, whither he voyaged for his health in quality of cook upon a Down-East schooner, was a man of letters, and had written a book to show the superiority of the black over the white branches of the human family. In this he held that, as all islands have been at their discovery found peopled by blacks, we must needs believe that humanity was first created of that color. Mrs. Johnson could not show us her husband's work (a sole copy in the library of an English gentleman at Port au Prince is not to be bought for money), but she often developed its arguments to the lady of the house; and one day, with a great show of reluctance, and many protests that no personal slight was meant, let fall the fact that Mr. Johnson believed the white race descended from Gehazi the leper, upon whom the leprosy of Naaman fell when the latter returned by Divine favor to his original black-ness. "And he went out from his presence a leper as white as snow," said Mrs. Johnson, quoting irrefutable Scripture. "Leprosy, leprosy," she added thoughtfully,— "nothing but leprosy bleached you out."

It seems to me much in her praise that she did not exult in our taint and degradation, as some white philosophers used to do in the opposite idea that a part of the human family were cursed to lasting blackness and slavery in Ham and his children, but even told us of a remarkable approach to whiteness in many of her own offspring. In a kindred spirit of charity, no doubt, she refused ever to attend church with people of her elder and wholesomer blood. When she went to church, she said, she always went to a white church, though while with us I am bound to say she never went to any. She professed to read her Bible in her bedroom on Sundays; but we suspected, from certain sounds and odors which used to steal out of this sanctuary, that her piety more commonly found expression in dozing and smoking.

I would not make a wanton jest here of Mrs. Johnson's anxiety to claim honor for the African color, while denying this color in many of her own family. It afforded a glimpse of the pain which all her people must endure, however proudly they hide it or light-heartedly forget it, from the despite and contumely to which they are guiltlessly born; and when I thought how irreparable was this disgrace and calamity of a black skin, and how irreparable it must be for ages yet, in this world where every other shame and all manner of wilful guilt and wickedness may hope for covert and pardon, I had little heart to laugh. Indeed, it was so pathetic to hear this poor old soul talk of her dead and lost ones, and try, in spite of all Mr. Johnson's theories and her own arrogant generalizations, to establish their whiteness, that we must have been very cruel and silly people to turn her sacred fables even into matter of question. I have no doubt that her Antoinette Anastasia and her Thomas Jefferson Wilberforce—it is impossible to give a full idea of the splendor and scope of the baptismal names in Mrs. Johnson's family—have as light skins and as golden hair in heaven as her reverend maternal fancy painted for them in our world. There, certainly, they would not be subject to tanning, which had ruined the delicate complexion, and had knotted into black woolly tangles the once wavy blonde locks of our little maid-servant Naomi; and I would fain believe that Toussaint Washington Johnson, who ran away to sea so many years ago, has found some fortunate zone where his hair and skin keep the same sunny and rosy tints they wore to his mother's eyes in infancy. But I have no means of knowing this, or of telling whether he was the prodigy of intellect that he was declared to be. Naomi could no more be taken in proof, of the one assertion than of the other. When she came to us, it was agreed that she should go to school; but she overruled her mother in this as in everything else, and never went. Except Sunday-school lessons, she had no other instruction than that her mistress gave her in the evenings, when a heavy day's play and the natural influences of the hour conspired with original causes to render her powerless before words of one syllable.

The first week of her service she was obedient and faithful to her duties; but, relaxing in the atmosphere of a house which seems to demoralize all menials, she shortly fell into disorderly ways of lying in wait for callers out of doors, and, when people rang, of running up the front steps, and letting them in from the outside. As the season expanded, and the fine weather became confirmed, she modified even this form of service, and spent her time in the fields, appearing at the house only when nature importunately craved molasses. She had a parrot-like quickness, so far as music was concerned, and learned from the Roman statuary to make the groves and half-finished houses resound,

"Camicia rossa,
Ove t' ascondi?
T' appella Italia,—
Tu non respondi!"

She taught the Garibaldi song, moreover, to all the neighboring children, so that I sometimes wondered if our street were not about to march upon Rome in a body.

In her untamable disobedience, Naomi alone betrayed her sylvan blood, for she was in all other respects negro and not Indian. But it was of her aboriginal ancestry that Mrs. Johnson chiefly boasted,—when not engaged in argument to maintain the superiority of the African race. She loved to descant upon it as the cause and explanation of her own

W. D. Howells

arrogant habit of feeling; and she seemed indeed to have inherited something of the Indian's hauteur along with the Ethiop's supple cunning and abundant amiability. She gave many instances in which her pride had met and overcome the insolence of employers, and the kindly old creature was by no means singular in her pride of being reputed proud.

She could never have been a woman of strong logical faculties, but she had in some things a very surprising and awful astuteness. She seldom introduced any purpose directly, but bore all about it and then suddenly sprung it upon her unprepared antagonist. At other times she obscurely hinted a reason, and left a conclusion to be inferred; as when she warded off reproach for some delinquency by saying in a general way that she had lived with ladies who used to come scolding into the kitchen after they had taken their bitters. "Quality ladies took their bitters regular," she added, to remove any sting of personality from her remark; for, from many things she had let fall, we knew that she did not regard us as quality. On the contrary, she often tried to overbear us with the gentility of her former places; and would tell the lady over whom she reigned, that she had lived with folks worth their three and four hundred thousand dollars, who never complained as she did of the ironing. Yet she had a sufficient regard for the literary occupations of the family, Mr. Johnson having been an author. She even professed to have herself written a book, which was still in manuscript, and preserved somewhere among her best clothes.

It was well, on many accounts, to be in contact with a mind so original and suggestive as Mrs. Johnson's. We loved to trace its intricate yet often transparent operations, and were perhaps too fond of explaining its peculiarities by facts of ancestry,—of finding hints of the Powwow or the Grand Custom in each grotesque development. We were conscious of something warmer in this old soul than in ourselves, and something wilder, and we chose to think it the tropic and the untracked forest. She had scarcely any being apart from her affection; she had no morality, but was good because she neither hated nor envied; and she might have been a saint far more easily than far more civilized people.

There was that also in her sinuous yet malleable nature, so full of guile and so full of goodness, that reminded us pleasantly of lowly folk in elder lands, where relaxing oppressions have lifted the restraints of fear between master and servant, without disturbing the familiarity of their relation. She advised freely with us upon all household matters, and took a motherly interest in whatever concerned us. She could be flattered or caressed into almost any service, but no threat or command could move her. When she erred, she never acknowledged her wrong in words, but handsomely expressed her regrets in a pudding, or sent up her apologies in a favorite dish secretly prepared. We grew so well used to this form of exculpation, that, whenever Mrs. Johnson took an afternoon at an inconvenient season, we knew that for a week afterwards we should be feasted like princes. She owned frankly that she loved us, that she never had done half so much for people before, and that she never had been nearly so well suited in any other place; and for a brief and happy time we thought that we never should part.

One day, however, our dividing destiny appeared in the basement, and was presented to us as Hippolyto Thucydides, the son of Mrs. Johnson, who had just arrived on a visit to his mother from the State of New Hampshire. He was a heavy and loutish youth, standing upon the borders of boyhood, and looking forward to the future with a vacant and listless eye. I mean that this was his figurative attitude; his actual manner, as he lolled

W. D. Howells

upon a chair beside the kitchen window, was so eccentric, that we felt a little uncertain how to regard him, and Mrs. Johnson openly described him as peculiar. He was so deeply tanned by the fervid suns of the New Hampshire winter, and his hair had so far suffered from the example of the sheep lately under his charge, that he could not be classed by any stretch of compassion with the blonde and straight-haired members of Mrs. Johnson's family.

He remained with us all the first day until late in the afternoon, when his mother took him out to get him a boarding-house. Then he departed in the van of her and Naomi, pausing at the gate to collect his spirits, and, after he had sufficiently animated himself by clapping his palms together, starting off down the street at a hand-gallop, to the manifest terror of the cows in the pastures, and the confusion of the less demonstrative people of our household. Other characteristic traits appeared in Hippolyto Thucydides within no very long period of time, and he ran away from his lodgings so often during the summer that he might be said to board round among the outlying corn-fields and turnip-patches of Charlesbridge. As a check upon this habit, Mrs. Johnson seemed to have invited him to spend his whole time in our basement; for whenever we went below we found him there, balanced— perhaps in homage to us, and perhaps as a token of extreme sensibility in himself—upon the low window-sill, the bottoms of his boots touching the floor inside, and his face buried in the grass without.

We could formulate no very tenable objection to all this, and yet the presence of Thucydides in our kitchen unaccountably oppressed our imaginations. We beheld him all over the house, a monstrous eidolon, balanced upon every window-sill; and he certainly attracted unplea-sant notice to our place, no less by his furtive and hang-dog manner of arrival than by the bold displays with which he celebrated his departures. We hinted this to Mrs. Johnson, but she could not enter into our feeling. Indeed, all the wild poetry of her maternal and primitive nature seemed to cast itself about this hapless boy; and if we had listened to her we should have believed there was no one so agreeable in society, or so quick-witted in affairs, as Hippolyto, when he chose. She used to rehearse us long epics concerning his industry, his courage, and his talent; and she put fine speeches in his mouth with no more regard to the truth than if she had been a historian, and not a poet. Perhaps she believed that he really said and did the things she attributed to him: it is the destiny of those who repeatedly tell great things either of themselves or others; and I think we may readily forgive the illusion to her zeal and fondness. In fact, she was not a wise woman, and she spoiled her children as if she had been a rich one.

At last, when we said positively that Thucydides should come to us no more, and then qualified the prohibition by allowing him to come every Sunday, she answered that she never would hurt the child's feelings by telling him not to come where his mother was; that people who did not love her children did not love her; and that, if Hippy went, she went. We thought it a master-stroke of firmness to rejoin that Hippolyto must go in any event; but I am bound to own that he did not go, and that his mother stayed, and so fed us with every cunning propitiatory dainty, that we must have been Pagans to renew our threat. In fact, we begged Mrs. Johnson to go into the country with us, and she, after long reluctation on Hippy's account, consented, agreeing to send him away to friends during her absence.

We made every preparation, and on the eve of our departure Mrs. Johnson went into the city to engage her son's passage to Bangor, while we awaited her return in untroubled security.

W. D. Howells

But she did not appear till midnight, and then responded with but a sad "Well, sah!" to the cheerful "Well, Mrs. Johnson!" that greeted her.

"All right, Mrs. Johnson?"

Mrs. Johnson made a strange noise, half chuckle and half death-rattle, in her throat. "All wrong, sah. Hippy's off again; and I've been all over the city after him."

"Then you can't go with us in the morning?"

"How *can* I, sah?"

Mrs. Johnson went sadly out of the room. Then she came back to the door again, and, opening it, uttered, for the first time in our service, words of apology and regret: "I hope I ha'n't put you out any. I *wanted* to go with you, but I ought to *knowed* I couldn't. All is, I loved you too much."

DOORSTEP ACQUAINTANCE

Vagabonds the world would no doubt call many of my doorstep acquaintance, and I do not attempt to defend them altogether against the world, which paints but black and white and in general terms. Yet I would fain veil what is only half-truth under another name, for I know that the service of their Gay Science is not one of such disgraceful ease as we associate with ideas of vagrancy, though I must own that they lead the life they do because they love it. They always protest that nothing but their ignorance of our tongue prevents them from practicing some mechanical trade. "What work could be harder," they ask, "than carrying this organ about all day?" but while I answer with honesty that nothing can be more irksome, I feel that they only pretend a disgust with it, and that they really like organ-grinding, if for no other reason than that they are the children of the summer, and it takes them into the beloved open weather. One of my friends, at least, who in the warmer months is to all appearance a blithesome troubadour, living

"A merry life in sun and shade,"

as a coal-heaver in winter; and though this more honorable and useful occupation is doubtless open to him the whole year round, yet he does not devote himself to it, but prefers with the expanding spring to lay aside his

W. D. Howells

grimy basket, and, shouldering his organ, to quit the dismal wharves and carts and cellars, and to wander forth into the suburbs, with his lazy, soft-eyed boy at his heels, who does nothing with his tambourine but take up a collection, and who, meeting me the other day in a chance passage of Ferry Street, knew me, and gave me so much of his father's personal history.

It was winter even there in Ferry Street, in which so many Italians live that one might think to find it under a softer sky and in a gentler air, and which I had always figured in a wide unlikeness to all other streets in Boston,—with houses stuccoed outside, and with gratings at their ground-floor windows; with mouldering archways between the buildings, and at the corners feeble lamps glimmering before pictures of the Madonna; with weather-beaten shutters flapping overhead, and many balconies from which hung the linen swathings of young infants, and love-making maidens furtively lured the velvet-jacketed, leisurely youth below: a place haunted by windy voices of blessing and cursing, with the perpetual clack of wooden-heeled shoes upon the stones, and what perfume from the blossom of vines and almond-trees, mingling with less delicate smells, the travelled reader pleases to imagine. I do not say that I found Ferry Street actually different from this vision in most respects; but as for the vines and almond-trees, they were not in bloom at the moment of my encounter with the little tambourine-boy. As we stood and talked, the snow fell as heavily and thickly around us as elsewhere in Boston. With a vague pain,—the envy of a race toward another born to a happier clime,—I heard from him that his whole family was going back to Italy in a month. The father had at last got together money enough, and the mother, who had long been an invalid, must be taken home; and, so far as I know, the population of Ferry Street exists but in the hope of a return, soon or late, to the native or the ancestral land.

More than one of my doorstep acquaintance, in fact, seemed to have no other stock in trade than this fond desire, and to thrive with it in our sympathetic community. It is scarcely possible but the reader has met the widow of Giovanni Cascamatto, a Vesuvian lunatic who has long set fire to their home on the slopes of the volcano, and perished in the flames. She was our first Italian acquaintance in Charlesbridge, presenting herself with a little subscription-book which she sent in for inspection, with a printed certificate to the facts of her history signed with the somewhat conventionally Saxon names of William Tompkins and John Johnson. These gentlemen set forth, in terms vaguer than can be reproduced, that her object in coming to America was to get money to go back to Italy; and the whole document had so fictitious an air that it made us doubt even the nationality of the bearer; but we were put to shame by the decent joy she manifested in an Italian salutation. There was no longer a question of imposture in anybody's mind; we gladly paid tribute to her poetic fiction, and she thanked us with a tranquil courtesy that placed the obligation where it belonged. As she turned to go with many good wishes, we pressed her to have some dinner, but she answered with a compliment insurpassably flattering, she had just dined—in another palace. The truth is, there is not a single palace on Benicia Street, and our little box of pine and paper would hardly have passed for a palace on the stage, where these things are often contrived with great simplicity; but as we had made a little Italy together, she touched it with the exquisite politeness of her race, and it became for the instant a lordly mansion, standing on the Chiaja, or the Via Nuovissima, or the Canalazzo.

I say this woman seemed glad to be greeted in Italian, but not, so far as I could see, surprised; and altogether the most amazing thing about my doorstep acquaintance of her nation is, that they are never surprised to be spoken to in their own tongue, or, if they are, never show it. A chestnut-roaster, who has sold me twice the chestnuts the same money would have bought of him in English, has not otherwise recognized the fact that Tuscan is not the dialect of Charlesbridge, and the mortifying nonchalance with which my advances have always been received has long since persuaded me that to the grinder at the gate it is not remarkable that a man should open the door of his wooden house on Benicia Street, and welcome him in his native language. After the first shock of this indifference is past, it is not to be questioned but it flatters with an illusion, which a stare of amazement would forbid, reducing the encounter to a vulgar reality at once, and I could almost believe it in those wily and amiable folk to intend the sweeter effect of their unconcern, which tacitly implies that there is no other tongue in the world but Italian, and which makes all the earth and air Italian for the time. Nothing else could have been the purpose of that image-dealer whom I saw on a summer's day lying at the foot of one of our meeting-houses, and doing his best to make it a cathedral, and really giving a sentiment of medieval art to the noble sculptures of the facade which the carpenters had just nailed up, freshly painted and newly repaired. This poet was stretched upon his back, eating, in that convenient posture, his dinner out of an earthen pot, plucking the viand from it, whatever it was, with his thumb and fore-finger, and dropping it piecemeal into his mouth. When the passer asked him "Where are you from?" he held a morsel in air long enough to answer "Da Lucca, signore," and then let it fall into his throat, and sank deeper into a reverie in which that crude accent even must have sounded like a gossip's or a kinsman's voice, but never otherwise moved muscle, nor looked to see who passed or lingered. There could have been little else in his circumstances to remind him of home, and if he was really in the sort of day-dream attributed to him, he was wise not to look about him. I have not myself been in Lucca, but I conceive that its piazza is not like our square, with a pump and horse-trough in the midst; but that it has probably a fountain and statuary, though not possibly so magnificent an elm towering above the bronze or marble groups as spreads its boughs of benison over our pump and the horse-car switchman, loitering near it to set the switch for the arriving cars, or lift the brimming buckets to the smoking nostrils of the horses, while out from the stable comes clanging and banging with a fresh team that famous African who has turned white, or, if he is off duty, one of his brethren who has not yet begun to turn. Figure, besides, an expressman watering his horse at the trough, a provision-cart backed up against the curb in front of one of the stores, various people looking from the car-office windows, and a conductor appearing at the door long enough to call out, "Ready for Boston!"—and you have a scene of such gayety as Lucca could never have witnessed in her piazza at high noon on a summer's day. Even our Campo Santo, if the Lucchese had cared to look round the corner of the meeting-house at its moss-grown head stones, could have had little to remind him of home, though it has antiquity and a proper quaintness. But not for him, not for them of his clime and faith, is the pathos of those simple memorial slates with their winged skulls, changing upon many later stones, as if by the softening of creeds and customs, to cherub's heads,—not for him is the pang I feel because of those who died, in our country's youth exiles or exiles' children, heirs of the wilderness and toil and hardship. Could they rise from their restful beds, and look on this wandering Italian with his plaster statuettes of Apollo, and Canovan dancers and deities, they would hold his wares little better than Romish saints and idolatries, and would scarcely have the sentimental interest in him felt by the modern citizen of Charlesbridge; but I think that even they must have respected that Lombard scissors-grinder who used to come to us, and put an edge to all the cutlery in the house.

He has since gone back to Milan, whence he came eighteen years ago, and whither he has returned,—as he told me one acute day in the fall, when all the winter hinted itself, and the painted leaves shuddered earthward in the grove across the way,—to enjoy a little climate before he died (*per goder un po' di dima prima di morire*). Our climate was the only thing he had against us; in every other respect he was a New-Englander, even to the early stages of consumption. He told me the story of his whole life, and of how in his adventurous youth he had left Milan and sojourned some years in Naples, vainly seeking his fortune there. Afterwards he went to Greece, and set up his ancestral business of greengrocer in Athens, faring there no better, but rather worse than in Naples, because of the deeper wickedness of the Athenians, who cheated him right and left, and whose laws gave him no redress. The Neapolitans were bad enough, he said, making a wry face, but the Greeks!—and he spat the Greeks out in the grass. At last, after much misfortune in Europe, he bethought him of coming to America, and he had never regretted it, but for the climate. You spent a good deal here,—nearly all you earned,—but then a poor man was a man, and the people were honest. It was wonderful to him that they all knew how to read and write, and he viewed with inexpressible scorn those Irish who came to this country, and were so little sensible of the benefits it conferred upon them. Boston he believed the best city in America, and "Tell me," said he, "is there such a thing anywhere else in the world as that Public Library?" He, a poor man, and almost unknown, had taken books from it to his own room, and was master to do so whenever he liked. He had thus been enabled to read Botta's history of the United States, an enormous compliment both to the country and the work which I doubt ever to have been paid before; and he knew more about Washington than I did, and desired to know more than I could tell him of the financial question among us. So we came to national politics, and then to European affairs. "It appears that Garibaldi will not go to Rome this year," remarks my scissors-grinder, who is very red in his sympathies. "The Emperor forbids! Well, patience! And that blessed Pope, what does he want, that Pope? He will be king find priest both, he will wear two pairs of shoes at once!" I must confess that no other of my door-step acquaintance had so clear an idea as this one of the difference between things here and at home. To the minds of most we seemed divided here as there into rich and poor,—*signori, persone eivili*, and *povera gente*,—and their thoughts about us did not go beyond a speculation as to our individual willingness or ability to pay for organ-grinding. But this Lombard was worthy of his adopted country, and I forgive him the frank expression of a doubt that one day occurred to him, when offered a glass of Italian wine. He held it daintily between him and the sun for a smiling moment, and then said, as if our wine must needs be as ungenuine as our Italian,—was perhaps some expression from the surrounding currant-bushes, harsh as that from the Northern tongues which could never give his language the true life and tonic charm,—"But I suppose this wine is not made of grapes, signor?" Yet he was a very courteous old man, elaborate in greeting and leave-taking, and with a quicker sense than usual. It was accounted delicacy in him, that, when he had bidden us a final adieu, he should never come near us again, though the date of his departure was postponed some weeks, and we heard him tinkling down the street, and stopping at the neighbors' houses. He was a keen-faced, thoughtful-looking man; and he wore a blouse of blue cotton, from the pocket of which always dangled the leaves of some wild salad culled from our wasteful vacant lots or prodigal waysides.

Altogether different in character was that Triestine, who came one evening to be helped home at the close of a very disastrous career in Mexico. He Was a person of innumerable bows, and fluttered his bright-colored compliments about, till it appeared that never before had such amiable people been asked charity by such a worthy and generous sufferer. In Trieste he had been a journalist, and it was evident enough from his speech that he was of a good education. He was vain of his Italian accent, which was peculiarly good for his heterogeneously peopled native city; and he made a show of that marvelous facility of the Triestines in languages, by taking me down French books, Spanish books, German books, and reading from them all with the properest accent. Yet with this boyish pride and self-satisfaction there was mixed a tone of bitter and worldly cynicism, a belief in fortune as the sole providence. As nearly as I could make out, he was a Johnson man in American politics; upon the Mexican question he was independent, disdaining French and Mexicans alike. He was with the former from the first, and had continued in the service of Maximilian after their withdrawal, till the execution of that prince made Mexico no place for adventurous merit. He was now going back to his native country, an ungrateful land enough, which had ill treated him long ago, but to which he nevertheless returned in a perfect gayety of temper. What a light-hearted rogue he was,—with such merry eyes, and such a pleasant smile shaping his neatly trimmed beard and mustache! After he had supped, and he Stood with us at the door taking leave, something happened to be said of Italian songs, whereupon this blithe exile, whom the compassion of strangers was enabling to go home after many years of unprofitable toil and danger to a country that had loved him not, fell to caroling a Venetian barcarole, and went sweetly away in its cadence. I bore him company as far as the gate of another Italian-speaking signor, and was there bidden adieu with great effusion, so that I forgot till he had left me to charge him not to be in fear of the house-dog, which barked but did not bite. In calling this after him, I had the misfortune to blunder in my verb. A man of another nation—perhaps another man of his own nation—would have cared rather for what I said than how I said it; but he, as if too zealous for the honor of his beautiful language to endure a hurt to it even in that moment of grief, lifting his hat, and bowing for the last time, responded with a "Morde, non morsica, signore!" and passed in under the pines, and next day to Italy.

There is a little old Genoese lady comes to sell us pins, needles, thread, tape, and the like *roba*, whom I regard as leading quite an ideal life in some respects. Her traffic is limited to a certain number of families who speak more or less Italian; and her days, so far as they are concerned, must be passed in an atmosphere of sympathy and kindliness. The truth is, we Northern and New World folk cannot help but cast a little romance about whoever comes to us from Italy, whether we have actually known the beauty and charm of that land or not. Then this old lady is in herself a very gentle and lovable kind of person, with a tender mother-face, which is also the face of a child. A smile plays always upon her wrinkled visage, and her quick and restless eyes are full of friendliness. There is never much stuff in her basket, however, and it is something of a mystery how she manages to live from it. None but an Italian could, I am sure; and her experience must test the full virtue of the national genius for cheap salads and much-extenuated soup-meat. I do not know whether it is native in her, or whether it is a grace acquired from long dealing with those kindly-hearted customers of hers in Charlesbridge, but she is of a most munificent spirit, and returns every smallest benefit with some present from her basket. She makes me ashamed of things I have written about the sordidness of her race, but I shall vainly seek to atone for them by open-handedness to her. She will give favor for favor; she will not even count the money she receives; our bargaining is a contest of the courtliest civilities, ending in many an "Adieu!" "To meet again!" "Remain well!" and "Finally!" not surpassed if rivaled in any Italian street. In her ineffectual way, she brings us news of her different customers, breaking up their stout Saxon names into tinkling polysyllables which suggest them only to the practiced sense, and is perfectly patient and contented if we mistake one for another. She loves them all, but she pities them as living in a terrible climate; and doubtless in her heart she purposes one day to go back to Italy, there to die. In the mean time she is very cheerful; she, too, has had her troubles,—what troubles I do not remember, but those that come by sickness and by death, and that really seem no sorrows until they come to us,—yet she never complains. It is hard to make a living, and the house-rent alone is six dollars a month; but still one lives, and does not fare so ill either. As it does not seem to be in her to dislike any one, it must be out of a harmless guile, felt to be comforting to servant-ridden householders, that she always speaks of "those Irish," her neighbors, with a bated breath, a shaken head, a hand lifted to the cheek, and an averted countenance.

Swarthiest of the organ-grinding tribe is he who peers up at my window out of infinitesimal black eyes, perceives me, louts low, and for form's sake grinds me out a tune before he begins to talk. As we parley together, say it is eleven o'clock in the forenoon, and a sober tranquillity reigns upon the dust and nodding weeds of Benicia Street. At that hour the organ-grinder and I are the only persons of our sex in the whole suburban population; all other husbands and fathers having eaten their breakfasts at seven o'clock, and stood up in the early horse-cars to Boston, whence they will return, with aching backs and quivering calves, half-pendant by leathern straps from the roofs of the same luxurious conveyances, in the evening. The Italian might go and grind his organ upon the front stoop of any one of a hundred French-roof houses around, and there would be no arm within strong enough to thrust him thence; but he is a gentleman in his way, and, as he prettily explains, he never stops to play except where the window smiles on him: a frowning lattice he will pass in silence. I behold in him a disappointed man,—a man broken in health, and of a liver baked by long sojourn in a tropical clime. In large and dim outline, made all the dimmer by his dialect, he sketches me the story of his life; how in his youth he ran away from the Milanese for love of a girl in France, who, dying, left him with so little purpose in the world that, after working at his trade of plasterer for some years in Lyons, he listened to a certain gentleman going out upon government service to a French colony in South America. This gentleman wanted a man-servant, and he said to my organ-grinder, "Go with me and I make your fortune." So he, who cared not whither he went, went, and found himself in the tropics. It was a hard life he led there; and of the wages that had seemed so great in France, he paid nearly half to his laundress alone, being forced to be neat in his master's house. The service was not so irksome in-doors, but it was the hunting beasts in the forest all day that broke his patience at last.

"Beasts in the forest?" I ask, forgetful of the familiar sense of *bestie*, and figuring cougars at least by the word.

"Yes, those little beasts for the naturalists,—flies, bugs, beetles,—Heaven knows what."

"But this brought you money?"

"It brought my master money, but me aches and pains as many as you will, and at last the fever. When that was burnt out, I made up my mind to ask for more pay, and, not getting it, to quit that service. I think the signor would have given it,—but the signora! So I left, empty as I came, and was cook on a vessel to New York."

This was the black and white of the man's story. I lose the color and atmosphere which his manner as well as his words bestowed upon it. He told it in a cheerful, impersonal kind of way as the romance of a poor devil which had interested him, and might possibly amuse me, leaving out no touch of character in his portrait of the fat, selfish master,—yielding enough, however, but for his grasping wife, who, with all her avarice and greed, he yet confessed to be very handsome. By the wave of a hand he housed them in a tropic residence, dim, cool, close shut, kept by servants in white linen moving with mute slippered feet over stone floors; and by another gesture he indicated the fierce thorny growths of the forest in which he hunted those vivid insects,—the luxuriant savannas, the gigantic ferns and palms, the hush and shining desolation, the presence of the invisible fever and death. There was a touch, too, of inexpressible sadness in his half-ignorant mention of the exiles at Cayenne, who were forbidden the wide ocean of escape about them by those swift gunboats keeping their coasts and swooping down upon every craft that left the shore. He himself had seen one such capture, and he made me see it, and the mortal despair of the fugitives, standing upright in their boat with the idle oars in their unconscious hands, while the corvette swept toward them.

For all his misfortunes, he was not cast down. He had that lightness of temper which seems proper to most northern Italians, whereas those from the south are usually dark-mooded, sad-faced men. Nothing surpasses for unstudied misanthropy of expression the visages of different Neapolitan harpers who have visited us; but they have some right to their dejected countenances as being of a yet half-civilized stock, and as real artists and men of genius. Nearly all wandering violinists, as well as harpers, are of their race, and they are of every age, from that of mere children to men in their prime. They are very rarely old, as many of the organ-grinders are; they are not so handsome as the Italians of the north, though they have invariably fine eyes. They arrive in twos and threes; the violinist briefly tunes his fiddle, and the harper unslings his instrument, and, with faces of profound gloom, they go through their repertory,—pieces from the great composers, airs from the opera, not unmingled with such efforts of Anglo-Saxon genius as Champagne Charley and Captain Jenks of the Horse Marines, which, like the language of Shakespeare and Milton, hold us and our English cousins in tender bonds of mutual affection. Beyond the fact that they come "dal Basilicat'," or "dal Principat'," one gets very little out of these Neapolitans, though I dare say they are not so surly at heart as they look. Money does not brighten them to the eye, but yet it touches them, and they are good in playing or leaving off to him that pays. Long time two of them stood between the gateway firs on a pleasant summer's afternoon and twanged and scraped their harmonious strings, till all the idle boys of the neighborhood gathered about them, listening with a grave and still delight. It was a most serious company: the Neapolitans, with their cloudy brows, rapt in their music; and the Yankee children, with their impassive faces, warily guarding against the faintest expression of enjoyment; and when at last the minstrels played a brisk measure, and the music began to work in the blood of the boys, and one of them shuffling his reluctant feet upon the gravel, broke into a sudden and resistless dance, the spectacle became too sad for contemplation. The boy danced only from the hips down; no expression of his face gave the levity sanction, nor did any of his comrades: they beheld him with a silent fascination, but none was infected by the solemn indecorum; and when the legs and music ceased their play together, no comment was made, and the dancer turned unheated away. A chance passer asked for what he called the Gearybaldeye Hymn, but the Neapolitans apparently did not know what this was.

My doorstep acquaintance were not all of one race; now and then an alien to the common Italian tribe appeared,— an Irish soldier, on his way to Salem, and willing to show me more of his mutilation than I cared to buy the sight of for twenty-five cents; and more rarely yet an American, also formerly of the army, but with something besides his wretchedness to sell. On the hottest day of last summer such a one rang the bell, and was discovered on the threshold wiping with his poor sole hand the sweat that stood upon his forehead. There was still enough of the independent citizen in his maimed and emaciated person to inspire him with deliberation and a show of that indifference with which we Americans like to encounter each other; but his voice was rather faint when he asked if I supposed we wanted any starch to-day.

"Yes, certainly," answered what heart there was within, taking note willfully, but I hope not wantonly, what an absurdly limp figure he was for a peddler of starch,— "certainly from you, brave fellow;" and the package being taken from his basket, the man turned to go away, so very wearily, that a cheap philanthropy protested: "For shame! ask him to sit down in-doors and drink a glass of water."

"No," answered the poor fellow, when this indignant voice had been obeyed, and he had been taken at a disadvantage, and as it were surprised into the confession, "my family hadn't any breakfast this morning, and I've got to hurry back to them."

"Haven't *you* had any breakfast?"

"Well, I wa'n't rightly hungry when I left the house."

"Here, now," popped in the virtue before named, "is an opportunity to discharge the debt we all owe to the brave fellows who gave us back our country. Make it beer."

So it was made beer and bread and cold meat, and, after a little pressing, the honest soul consented to the refreshment. He sat down in a cool doorway and began to eat and to tell of the fight before Vicksburg. And if you have never seen a one-armed soldier making a meal, I can assure you the sight is a pathetic one, and is rendered none the cheerfuller by his memories of the fights that mutilated him. This man had no very susceptible audience, but before he was carried off the field, shot through the body, and in the arm and foot, he had sold every package of starch in his basket. I am ashamed to say this now, for I suspect that a man with one arm, who indulged himself in going about under that broiling sun of July, peddling starch, was very probably an impostor. He computed a good day's profits of seventy-five cents, and when asked if that was not very little for the support of a sick wife and three children, he answered with a quaint effort at impressiveness, and with a trick, as I imagined, from the manner of the regimental chaplain, "You've done your duty, my friend, and more'n your duty. If every one did their duty like that, we should get along." So he took leave, and shambled out into the furnace-heat, the sun beating upon his pale face, and his linen coat hugging him close, but with his basket lighter, and I hope his heart also. At any rate, this was the sentiment which cheap philanthropy offered in self-gratulation, as he passed out of sight: "There! you are quits with those maimed soldiers at last, and you have a country which you have paid for with cold victuals as they with blood."

We have been a good deal visited by one disbanded

volunteer, not to the naked eye maimed, nor apparently suffering from any lingering illness, yet who bears, as he tells me, a secret disabling wound in his side from a spent shell, and who is certainly a prey to the most acute form of shiftlessness. I do not recall with exactness the date of our acquaintance, but it was one of those pleasant August afternoons when a dinner eaten in peace fills the digester with a millennial tenderness for the race too rarely felt in the nineteenth century. At such a moment it is a more natural action to loosen than to tighten the purse-strings, and when a very neatly dressed young man presented himself at the gate, and, in a note of indescribable plaintiveness, asked if I had any little job for him to do that he might pay for a night's lodging, I looked about the small domain with a vague longing to find some part of it in disrepair, and experienced a moment's absurd relief when he hinted that he would be willing to accept fifty cents in pledge of future service. Yet this was not the right principle: some work, real or apparent, must be done for the money, and the veteran was told that he might weed the strawberry bed, though, as matters then stood, it was clean enough for a strawberry bed that never bore anything. The veteran was neatly dressed, as I have said: his coat, which was good, was buttoned to the throat for reasons that shall be sacred against curiosity, and he had on a perfectly clean paper collar; he was a handsome young fellow, with regular features, and a solicitously kept imperial and mustache; his hair, when he lifted his hat, appeared elegantly oiled and brushed. I did not hope from this figure that the work done would be worth the money paid, and, as nearly as I can compute, the weeds he took from that bed cost me a cent apiece, to say nothing of a cup of tea given him in grace at the end of his labors.

My acquaintance was, as the reader will be glad to learn, a native American, though it is to be regretted, for the sake of facts which his case went far to establish, that he was not a New-Englander by birth. The most that could be claimed was, that he came to Boston from Delaware when very young, and that there on that brine-washed granite he had grown as perfect a flower of helplessness and indolence, as fine a fruit of maturing civilization, as ever expanded or ripened in Latin lands. He lived, not only a protest in flesh and blood against the tendency of democracy to exclude mere beauty from our system, but a refutation of those Old World observers, who deny to our vulgar and bustling communities the refining and elevating grace of Repose. There was something very curious and original in his character, from which the sentiment of shame was absent, but which was not lacking in the fine instincts of personal cleanliness, of dress, of style. There was nothing of the rowdy in him; he was gentle as an Italian noble in his manners: what other traits they may have had in common, I do not know; perhaps an amiable habit of illusion. He was always going to bring me his discharge papers, but he never did, though he came often and had many a pleasant night's sleep at my cost. If sometimes he did a little work, he spent great part of the time contracted to me in the kitchen, where it was understood, quite upon his own agency, that his wages included board. At other times, he called for money too late in the evening to work it out that day, and it has happened that a new second girl, deceived by his genteel appearance in the uncertain light, has shown him into the parlor, where I have found him to his and my own great amusement, as the gentleman who wanted to see me. Nothing else seemed to raise his ordinarily dejected spirits so much. We all know how pleasant it is to laugh at people behind their backs; but this veteran afforded me at a very low rate the luxury of a fellow-being whom one might laugh at to his face as much as one liked.

Yet with all his shamelessness, his pensiveness, his elegance, I felt that somehow our national triumph was not complete in him,—that there were yet more finished forms of self-abasement in the Old World, till one day I looked out of the window and saw at a little distance my veteran digging a cellar for an Irishman. I own that the spectacle gave me a shock of pleasure, and that I ran down to have a nearer view of what human eyes have seldom, if ever, beheld,—an American, pure blood, handling the pick, the shovel, and the wheelbarrow, while an Irishman directed his labors. Upon inspection, it appeared that none of the trees grew with their roots in the air, in recognition of this great reversal of the natural law; all the French-roof houses stood right side up. The phenomenon may become more common in future, unless the American race accomplishes its destiny of dying out before the more populatory foreigner, but as yet it graced the veteran with an exquisite and signal distinction. He, however, seemed to feel unpleasantly the anomaly of his case, and opened the conversation by saying that he should not work at that job to-morrow, it hurt his side; and went on to complain of the inhumanity of Americans to Americans. "Why," said he, "they'd rather give out their jobs to a nigger than to one of their own kind. I was beatin' carpets for a gentleman on the Avenue, and the first thing I know he give most of 'em to a nigger. I beat seven of 'em in one day, and got two dollars; and the nigger beat 'em by the piece, and he got a dollar an' a half apiece. My luck!"

Here the Irishman glanced at his hireling, and the rueful veteran hastened to pile up another wheelbarrow with earth. If ever we come to reverse positions generally with our Irish brethren, there is no doubt but they will get more work out of us than we do from them at present.

It was shortly after this that the veteran offered to do second girl's work in my house if I would take him. The place was not vacant; and as the summer was now drawing to a close, and I feared to be left with him on my hands for the winter, it seemed well to speak to him upon the subject of economy. The next time he called, I had not about me the exact sum for a night's lodging,—fifty cents, namely—and asked him if he thought a dollar would do He smiled sadly, as if he did not like jesting upon such a very serious subject, but said he allowed to work it out, and took it.

"Now, I hope you won't think I am interfering with your affairs," said his benefactor, "but I really think you are a very poor financier. According to your own account, you have been going on from year to year for a long time, trusting to luck for a night's lodging. Sometimes I suppose you have to sleep out-of-doors."

"No, never!" answered the veteran, with something like scorn. "I never sleep out-doors. I wouldn't do it."

"Well, at any rate, some one has to pay for your lodging. Don't you think you'd come cheaper to your friends, if, instead of going to a hotel every night, you'd take a room somewhere, and pay for it by the month?"

"I've thought of that. If I could get a good bed, I'd try it awhile anyhow. You see the hotels have raised. I used to get a lodgin' and a nice breakfast for a half a dollar, but now it is as much as you can do to get a lodgin' for the money, and it's just as dear in the Port as it is in the city. I've tried hotels pretty much everywhere, and one's about as bad as another."

If he had been a travelled Englishman writing a book, he could not have spoken of hotels with greater disdain.

"You see, the trouble with me is, I ain't got any relations around here. Now," he added, with the life and eagerness of an inspiration, "if I had a mother and sister livin' down at the Port, say, I wouldn't go hunting about for these mean little jobs everywheres. I'd just lay round home, and wait till something come up big. What I want is a home."

At the instigation of a malignant spirit I asked the homeless orphan, "Why don't you get married, then?"

He gave me another smile, sadder, fainter, sweeter than before, and said: "When would you like to see me again, so I could work out this dollar?"

A sudden and unreasonable disgust for the character which had given me so much entertainment succeeded to my past delight. I felt, moreover, that I had bought the right to use some frankness with the veteran, and I said to him: "Do you know now, I shouldn't care if I *never* saw you again?"

I can only conjecture that he took the confidence in good part, for he did not appear again after that.

A PEDESTRIAN TOUR

Walking for walking's sake I do not like. The diversion appears to me one of the most factitious of modern enjoyments; and I cannot help looking upon those who pace their five miles in the teeth of a north wind, and profess to come home all the livelier and better for it, as guilty of a venial hypocrisy. It is in nature that after such an exercise the bones should ache and the flesh tremble; and I suspect that these harmless pretenders are all the while paying a secret penalty for their bravado. With a pleasant end in view, or with cheerful companionship, walking is far from being the worst thing in life; though doubtless a truly candid person must confess that he would rather ride under the same circumstances. Yet it is certain that some sort of recreation is necessary after a day spent within doors; and one is really obliged nowadays to take a little walk instead of medicine; for one's doctor is sure to have a mania on the subject, and there is no more getting pills or powders out of him for a slight indigestion than if they had all been shot away at the rebels during the war. For this reason I sometimes go upon a pedestrian tour, which is of no great extent in itself, and which I moreover modify by keeping always within sound of the horse-car bells, or easy reach of some steam-car station.

I fear that I should find these rambles dull, but that their

W. D. Howells

utter lack of interest amuses me. I will be honest with the reader, though, and any Master Pliable is free to forsake me at this point; for I cannot promise to be really livelier than my walk. There is a Slough of Despond in full view, and not a Delectable Mountain to be seen, unless you choose so to call the high lands about Waltham, which we shall behold dark blue against the western sky presently. As I sally forth upon Benicia Street, the whole suburb of Charlesbridge stretches about me,—a vast space upon which I can embroider any fancy I like as I saunter along. I have no associations with it, or memories of it, and, at some seasons, I might wander for days in the most frequented parts of it, and meet hardly any one I know. It is not, however, to these parts that I commonly turn, but northward, up a street upon which a flight of French-roof houses suddenly settled a year or two since, with families in them, and many outward signs of permanence, though their precipitate arrival might cast some doubt upon this. I have to admire their uniform neatness and prettiness, and I look at their dormer-windows with the envy of one to whose weak sentimentality dormer-windows long appeared the supreme architectural happiness. But, for all my admiration of the houses, I find a variety that is pleasanter in the landscape, when I reach, beyond them, a little bridge which appears to span a small stream. It unites banks lined with a growth of trees and briers nodding their heads above the neighboring levels, and suggesting a quiet water-course, though in fact it is the Fitchburg Railroad that purls between them, with rippling freight and passenger trains and ever-gurgling loco- motives. The banks take the earliest green of spring upon their southward slope, and on a Sunday morning of May, when the bells are lamenting the Sabbaths of the past, I find their sunny tranquillity sufficient to give me a slight heart-ache for I know not what. If I descend them and follow the railroad westward half a mile, I come to vast brick-yards, which are not in themselves exciting to the

imagination, and which yet, from an irresistible association of ideas, remind me of Egypt, and are forever
newly forsaken of those who made bricks without straw;
so that I have no trouble in erecting temples and dynastic
tombs out of the kilns; while the mills for grinding the
clay serve me very well for those sad-voiced *sakias* or
wheel-pumps which the Howadji Curtis heard wailing at
their work of drawing water from the Nile. A little farther
on I come to the boarding-house built at the railroad side
for the French Canadians who have by this time
succeeded the Hebrews in the toil of the brick-yards, and
who, as they loiter in windy-voiced, good-humored
groups about the doors of their lodgings, insist upon
bringing before me the town of St. Michel at the mouth of
the great Mont Cenis tunnel, where so many peasant folk
like them are always amiably quarreling before the
cabarets when the diligence comes and goes. Somewhere,
there must be a gendarme with a cocked hat and a sword
on, standing with folded arms to represent the Empire and
Peace among that rural population; if I looked in-doors, I
am sure I should see the neatest of landladies and
landladies' daughters and nieces in high black silk caps,
bearing hither and thither smoking bowls of *bouillon* and
cafe-au-lait. Well, it takes as little to make one happy as
miserable, thank Heaven! and I derive a cheerfulness
from this scene which quite atones to me for the fleeting
desolation suffered from the sunny verdure on the railroad
bank. With repaired spirits I take my way up through the
brick-yards towards the Irish settlement on the north,
passing under the long sheds that shelter the kilns. The
ashes lie cold about the mouths of most, and the bricks are
burnt to the proper complexion; in others these are freshly
arranged over flues in which the fire has not been kindled;
but in whatever state I see them, I am reminded of brick-
kilns of boyhood. They were then such palaces of
enchantment as any architect should now vainly attempt
to rival with bricks upon the most desirable corner lot of

the Back Bay, and were the homes of men truly to be envied: men privileged to stay up all night; to sleep, as it were, out of doors; to hear the wild geese as they flew over in the darkness; to be waking in time to shoot the early ducks that visited the neighboring ponds; to roast corn upon the ends of sticks; to tell and to listen to stories that never ended, save in some sudden impulse to rise and dance a happy hoe-down in the ruddy light of the kiln-fires. If by day they were seen to have the redness of eyes of men that looked upon the whiskey when it was yellow and gave its color in the flask; if now and then the fragments of a broken bottle strewed the scene of their vigils, and a head broken to match appeared among those good comrades, the boyish imagination was not shocked by these things, but accepted them merely as the symbols of a free virile life. Some such life no doubt is still to be found in the Dublin to which I am come by the time my repertory of associations with brick-kilns is exhausted, but, oddly enough, I no longer care to encounter it.

It is perhaps in a pious recognition of our mortality that Dublin is built around the Irish grave-yard. Most of its windows look out upon the sepulchral monuments and the pretty constant arrival of the funeral trains with their long lines of carriages bringing to the celebration of the sad ultimate rites those gay companies of Irish mourners. I suppose that the spectacle of such obsequies is not at all depressing to the inhabitants of Dublin; but that, on the contrary, it must beget in them a feeling which, if not resignation to death, is, at least, a sort of sub-acute cheerfulness in his presence. None but a Dubliner, however, would have been greatly animated by a scene which I witnessed during a stroll through this cemetery one afternoon of early spring. The fact that a marble slab or shaft more or less sculptured, and inscribed with words more or less helpless, is the utmost that we can give to one whom once we could caress with every tenderness of speech and touch, and that, after all, the memorial we raise is rather to our own grief, and is a decency, a mere conventionality,—this is a dreadful fact on which the heart breaks itself with such a pang, that it always seems a desolation never recognized, an anguish never felt before. Whilst I stood revolving this thought in my mind, and reading the Irish names upon the stones and the black head-boards,—the latter adorned with pictures of angels, once gilt, but now weather-worn down to the yellow paint,—a wail of intolerable pathos filled the air: "O my darling, O my darling! O—O—O!" with sobs and groans and sighs; and, looking about, I saw two women, one standing upright beside another that had cast herself upon a grave, and lay clasping it with her comfortless arms, uttering these cries. The grave was a year old at least, but the grief seemed of yesterday or of that morning. At times the friend that stood beside the prostrate woman stooped and spoke a soothing word to her, while she wailed out her woe; and in the midst some little ribald Irish boys came scuffling and quarreling up the pathway, singing snatches of an obscene song; and when both the wailing and the singing had died away, an old woman, decently clad, and with her many-wrinkled face softened by the old-fashioned frill running round the inside of her cap, dropped down upon her knees beside a very old grave, and clasped her hands in a silent prayer above it.

If I had beheld all this in some village *campo santo* in Italy, I should have been much more vividly impressed by it, as an aesthetical observer; whereas I was now merely touched as a human being, and had little desire to turn the scene to literary account. I could not help feeling that it wanted the atmosphere of sentimental association, the whole background was a blank or worse than a blank. Yet I have not been able to hide from myself so much as I would like certain points of resemblance between our Irish and the poorer classes of Italians. The likeness is one

W. D. Howells

of the first things that strikes an American in Italy, and I am always reminded of it in Dublin. So much of the local life appears upon the street; there is so much gossip from house to house, and the talk is always such a resonant clamoring; the women, bareheaded, or with a shawl folded over the head and caught beneath the chin with the hand, have such a contented down-at-heel aspect, shuffling from door to door, or lounging, arms akimbo, among the cats and poultry at their own thresholds, that one beholding it all might well fancy himself upon some Italian *calle* or *vicolo*. Of course the illusion does not hold good on a Sunday, when the Dubliners are coming home from church in their best,—their extraordinary best bonnets and their prodigious silk hats. It does not hold good in any way or at any time, except upon the surface, for there is beneath all this resemblance the difference that must exist between a race immemorially civilized and one which has lately emerged from barbarism "after six centuries of oppression." You are likely to find a polite pagan under the mask of the modern Italian you feel pretty sure that any of his race would with a little washing and skillful manipulation, *restore*, like a neglected painting, into something genuinely graceful and pleasing; but if one of these Yankeefied Celts were scraped, it is but too possible that you might find a kern, a Whiteboy, or a Pikeman. The chance of discovering a scholar or a saint of the period when Ireland was the centre of learning, and the favorite seat of the Church, is scarcely one in three.

Among the houses fronting on the main street of Dublin, every other one—I speak in all moderation—is a grocery, if I may judge by a tin case of corn-balls, a jar of candy, and a card of shirt-buttons, with an under layer of primers and ballads, in the windows. You descend from the street by several steps into these haunts, which are contrived to secure the greatest possible dampness and darkness; and if you have made an errand inside, you doubtless find a lady before the counter in the act of putting down a guilty-looking tumbler with one hand, while she neatly wipes her mouth on the back of the other. She has that effect, observable in all tippling women of low degree, of having no upper garment on but a shawl, which hangs about her in statuesque folds and lines. She slinks out directly, but the lady behind the counter gives you good evening with

"The affectation of a bright-eyed ease,"

intended to deceive if you chance to be a State constable in disguise, and to propitiate if you are a veritable customer: "Who was that woman, lamenting so, over in the grave-yard?" "O, I don't know, sir," answered the lady, making change for the price of a ballad. "Some Irish folks. They ginerally cries that way."

In yet earlier spring walks through Dublin, I found a depth of mud appalling even to one who had lived three years in Charlesbridge. The streets were passable only to pedestrians skilled in shifting themselves along the sides of fences and alert to take advantage of every projecting doorstep. There were no dry places, except in front of the groceries, where the ground was beaten hard by the broad feet of loafing geese and the coming and going of admirably small children making purchases there. The number of the little ones was quite as remarkable as their size, and ought to have been even more interesting, if, as sometimes appears probable, such increase shall— together with the well-known ambition of Dubliners to rule the land—one day make an end of us poor Yankees as a dominant plurality.

The town was somewhat tainted with our architectural respectability, unless the newness of some of the buildings gave illusion of this; and, though the streets of Dublin were not at all cared for, and though every house on the main thoroughfare stood upon the brink of a slough, without yard, or any attempt at garden or shrubbery, there were many cottages in the less aristocratic quarters inclosed in palings, and embowered in the usual suburban pear-trees and currant-bushes. These, indeed, were dwellings of an elder sort, and had clearly been inherited from a population now as extinct in that region as the Pequots, and they were not always carefully cherished. On the border of the hamlet is to be seen an old farm-house of the poorer sort, built about the beginning of this century, and now thickly peopled by Dubliners. Its gate is thrown down, and the great wild-grown lilac hedge, no longer protected by a fence, shows skirts bedabbled by the familiarity of lawless poultry, as little like the steady-habited poultry of other times, as the people of the house are like the former inmates, long since dead or gone West. I offer the poor place a sentiment of regret as I pass, thinking of its better days. I think of its decorous, hard-working, cleanly, school-going, church-attending life, which was full of the pleasure of duty done, and was not without its own quaint beauty and grace. What long Sabbaths were kept in that old house, what scanty holidays! Yet from this and such as this came the dominion of the whole wild continent, the freedom of a race, the greatness of the greatest people. It may be that I regretted a little too exultantly, and that out of this particular house came only peddling of innumerable clocks and multitudinous tin-ware. But as yet, it is pretty certain that the general character of the population has not gained by the change. What is in the future, let the prophets say; any one can see that something not quite agreeable is in the present; something that takes the wrong side, as by instinct, in politics; something that mainly helps to prop up tottering priestcraft among us; something that one thinks of with dismay as destined to control so largely the civil and religious interests of the country. This, however, is only the aggregate aspect. Mrs.

Clannahan's kitchen, as it may be seen by the desperate philosopher when he goes to engage her for the spring house-cleaning, is a strong argument against his fears. If Mrs. Clannahan, lately of an Irish cabin, can show a kitchen so capably appointed and so neatly kept as that, the country may yet be an inch or two from the brink of ruin, and the race which we trust as little as we love may turn out no more spendthrift than most heirs. It is encouraging, moreover, when any people can flatter themselves upon a superior prosperity and virtue, and we may take heart from the fact that the French Canadians, many of whom have lodgings in Dublin, are not well seen by the higher classes of the citizens there. Mrs. Clannahan, whose house stands over against the main gate of the grave-yard, and who may, therefore, be considered as moving in the best Dublin society, hints, that though good Catholics, the French are not thought perfectly honest,—"things have been missed" since they came to blight with their crimes and vices the once happy seat of integrity. It is amusing to find Dublin fearful of the encroachment of the French, as we, in our turn, dread the advance of the Irish. We must make a jest of our own alarms, and even smile—since we cannot help our-selves—at the spiritual desolation occasioned by the settlement of an Irish family in one of our suburban neighborhoods. The householders view with fear and jealousy the erection of any dwelling of less than a stated cost, as portending a possible advent of Irish; and when the calamitous race actually appears, a mortal pang strikes to the bottom of every pocket. Values tremble throughout that neighborhood, to which the new-comers commu-nicate a species of moral dry-rot. None but the Irish will build near the Irish; and the infection of fear spreads to the elder Yankee homes about, and the owners prepare to abandon them,—not always, however, let us hope, without turning, at the expense of the invaders, a Parthian penny in their flight. In my walk from Dublin to North

Charlesbridge, I saw more than one token of the encroachment of the Celtic army, which had here and there invested a Yankee house with besieging shanties on every side, and thus given to its essential and otherwise quite hopeless ugliness a touch of the poetry that attends failing fortunes, and hallows decayed gentility of however poor a sort originally. The fortunes of such a house are, of course, not to be retrieved. Where the Celt sets his foot, there the Yankee (and it is perhaps wholesome if not agreeable to know that the Irish citizen whom we do not always honor as our equal in civilization loves to speak of us scornfully as Yankees) rarely, if ever, returns. The place remains to the intruder and his heirs forever. We gracefully retire before him even in politics, as the metropolis—if it is the metropolis—can witness; and we wait with an anxious curiosity the encounter of the Irish and the Chinese, now rapidly approaching each other from opposite shores of the continent. Shall we be crushed in the collision of these superior races? Every intelligence-office will soon be ringing with the cries of combat, and all our kitchens strewn with pig-tails and bark chignons. As yet we have gay hopes of our Buddhistic brethren; but how will it be when they begin to quarter the Dragon upon the Stars and Stripes, and buy up all the best sites for temples, and burn their joss-sticks, as it were, under our very noses? Our grasp upon the great problem grows a little lax, perhaps? Is it true that, when we look so anxiously for help from others, the virtue has gone out of ourselves? I should hope not.

As I leave Dublin, the houses grow larger and handsomer; and as I draw near the Avenue, the Mansard-roofs look down upon me with their dormer-windows, and welcome me back to the American community. There are fences about all the houses, inclosing ampler and ampler door-yards; the children, which had swarmed in the thriftless and unenlightened purlieus of Dublin, diminish in number and finally disappear; the chickens have vanished; and I hear—I hear the pensive music of the horse-car bells, which in some alien land, I am sure, would be as pathetic to me as the Ranz des Vaches to the Swiss or the bagpipes to the Highlander: in the desert, where the traveller seems to hear the familiar bells of his far-off church, this tinkle would haunt the absolute silence, and recall the exile's fancy to Charlesbridge; and perhaps in the mocking mirage he would behold an airy horse-car track, and a phantasmagoric horse-car moving slowly along the edge of the horizon, with spectral passengers closely packed inside and overflowing either platform.

But before I reach the Avenue, Dublin calls to me yet again, in the figure of an old, old man, wearing the clothes of other times, and a sort of ancestral round hat. In the act of striking a match he asks me the time of day, and, applying the fire to his pipe, he returns me his thanks in a volume of words and smoke. What a wrinkled and unshorn old man! Can age and neglect do so much for any of us? This ruinous person was associated with a hand-cart as decrepit as himself, but not nearly so cheerful; for though he spoke up briskly with a spirit uttered from far within the wrinkles and the stubble, the cart had preceded him with a very lugubrious creak. It groaned, in fact, under a load of tin cans, and I was to learn from the old man that there was, and had been, in his person, for thirteen years, such a thing in the world as a peddler of buttermilk, and that these cans were now filled with that pleasant drink. They did not invite me to prove their contents, being cans that apparently passed their vacant moments in stables and even manure-heaps, and that looked somehow emulous of that old man's stubble and wrinkles. I bought nothing, but I left the old peddler well content, seated upon a thill of his cart, smoking tranquilly, and filling the keen spring evening air with fumes which it dispersed abroad, and made to itself a pleasant incense of.

I left him a whole epoch behind, as I entered the Avenue and lounged homeward along the stately street. Above the station it is far more picturesque than it is below, and the magnificent elms that shadow it might well have looked, in their saplinghood, upon the British straggling down the country road from the Concord fight; and there are some ancient houses yet standing that must have been filled with exultation at the same spectacle. Poor old revolutionaries! they would never have believed that their descendants would come to love the English as we do.

The season has advanced rapidly during my progress from Dublin to the Avenue; and by the time I reach the famous old tavern, not far from the station, it is a Sunday morning of early summer, and the yellow sunlight falls upon a body of good comrades who are grooming a marvelous number of piebald steeds about the stable-doors. By token of these beasts—which always look so much more like works of art than of nature—I know that there is to be a circus somewhere very soon; and the gay bills pasted all over the stable-front tell me that there are to be two performances at the Port on the morrow. The grooms talk nothing and joke nothing but horse at their labor; and their life seems such a low, ignorant, happy life, that the secret nomad lurking in every respectable and stationary personality stirs within me and struggles to strike hands of fellowship with them. They lead a sort of pastoral existence in our age of railroads; they wander over the continent with their great caravan, and everywhere pursue the summer from South to North and from North to South again; in the mild forenoons they groom their herds, and in the afternoons they doze under their wagons, indifferent to the tumult of the crowd within and without the mighty canvas near them,—doze face downwards on the bruised, sweet-smelling grass; and in the starry midnight rise and strike their tents, and set forth again over the still country roads, to take the next village on the morrow with the blaze and splendor of their "Grand Entree." The triumphal chariot in which the musicians are borne at the head of the procession is composed, as I perceive by the bills, of four colossal gilt swans, set tail to tail, with lifted wings and curving necks; but the chariot, as I behold it beside the stable, is mysteriously draped in white canvas, through which its gilding glitters only here and there. And does it move thus shrouded in the company's wanderings from place to place, and is the precious spottiness of the piebalds then hidden under envious drapery? O happy grooms,—not clean as to shirts, nor especially neat in your conversation, but displaying a Wealth of art in India-ink upon your manly chests and the swelling muscles of your arms, and speaking in every movement your freedom from all conventional gyves and shackles, *"seid umschlungen!"*—in spirit; for the rest, you are rather too damp, and seem to have applied your sudsy sponges too impartially to your own trousers and the horses' legs to receive an actual embrace from a *dilettante* vagabond.

The old tavern is old only comparatively; but in our new and changeful life it is already quaint. It is very long, and low-studded in either story, with a row of windows in the roof, and a great porch, furnished with benches, running the whole length of the ground-floor. Perhaps because they take the dust of the street too freely, or because the guests find it more social and comfortable to gather in-doors in the wide, low-ceiled office, the benches are not worn, nor particularly whittled. The room has the desolate air characteristic of offices which have once been bar-rooms; but no doubt, on a winter's night, there is talk worth listening to there, of flocks, and herds and horse-trades, from the drovers and cattle-market men who patronize the tavern; and the artistic temperament, at least, could feel no regret if that sepulchrally penitent bar-room then developed a secret capacity for the wickedness that once boldly glittered behind the counter in rows of decanters.

The house was formerly renowned for its suppers, of which all that was learned or gifted in the old college town of Charlesbridge used to partake; and I have heard lips which breathe the loftiest song and the sweetest humor—let alone being "dewy with the Greek of Plato"—smacked regretfully over the memory of those suppers' roast and broiled. No such suppers, they say, are cooked in the world any more; and I am somehow made to feel that their passing away is connected with the decay of good literature.

I hope it may be very long before the predestined French-roof villa occupies the tavern's site, and turns into lawns and gardens its wide-spreading cattle-pens, and removes the great barn that now shows its broad, low gable to the street. This is yet older and quainter-looking than the tavern itself; it is mighty capacious, and gives a still profounder impression of vastness with its shed, of which the roof slopes southward down almost to a man's height from the ground, and shelters a row of mangers, running back half the length of the stable, and serving in former times for the baiting of such beasts as could not be provided for within. But the halcyon days of the cattle-market are past (though you may still see the white horns tossing above the fences of the pens, when a newly arrived herd lands from the train to be driven afoot to Brighton), and the place looks now so empty and forsaken, spite of the circus baggage-wagons, that it were hard to believe these mangers could ever have been in request, but for the fact that they are all gnawed, down to the quick as it were, by generations of horses—vanished forever on the deserted highways of the past—impatient for their oats or hungering for more.

The day must come, of course, when the mangers will all be taken from the stable-shed, and exposed for sale at that wonderful second-hand shop which stands over against the tavern. I am no more surprised than one in a dream, to find it a week-day afternoon by the time I have crossed thither from the circus-men grooming their piebalds. It is an enchanted place to me, and I am a frequent and unprofitable customer there, buying only just enough to make good my footing with the custodian of its marvels, who is, of course, too true an American to show any desire to sell. Without, on either side of the doorway, I am pretty sure to find, among other articles of furniture, a mahogany and hair-cloth sofa, a family portrait, a landscape painting, a bath-tub, and a flower-stand, with now and then the variety of a boat and a dog-house; while under an adjoining shed is heaped a mass of miscellaneous movables, of a heavier sort, and fearlessly left there night and day, being on all accounts undesirable to steal. The door of the shop rings a bell in opening, and ushers the customer into a room which Chaos herself might have planned in one of her happier moments. Carpets, blankets, shawls, pictures, mirrors, rocking-chairs, and blue overalls hang from the ceiling, and devious pathways wind amidst piles of ready-made clothing, show-cases filled with every sort of knick-knack and half hidden under heaps of hats and boots and shoes, bookcases, secretaries, chests of drawers, mattresses, lounges, and bedsteads, to the stairway of a loft similarly appointed, and to a back room overflowing with glassware and crockery. These things are not all second-hand, but they are all old and equally pathetic. The melancholy of ruinous auction sales, of changing tastes or changing fashions, clings to them, whether they are things that have never had a home and have been on sale ever since they were made, or things that have been associated with every phase of human life.

Among other objects, certain large glass vases, ornamented by the polite art of potichomanie, have long
appealed to my fancy, wherein they capriciously allied
themselves to the history of aging single women in lonely
New England village houses,—pathetic sisters lingering
upon the neutral ground between the faded hopes of
marriage and the yet unrisen prospects of consumption.
The work implies an imperfect yet real love of beauty, the
leisure for it a degree of pecuniary ease: the thoughts of
the sisters rise above the pickling and preserving that
occupied their heartier and happier mother; they are in
fact in that aesthetic, social, and intellectual mean, in
which single women are thought soonest to wither and
decline. With a little more power, and in our later era,
they would be writing stories full of ambitious,
unintelligible, self-devoted and sudden collapsing young
girls and amazing doctors; but as they are, and in their
time, they must do what they can. A sentimentalist may
discern on these vases not only the gay designs with
which they ornamented them, but their own dim faces
looking wan from the windows of some huge old
homestead, a world too wide for the shrunken family. All
April long the door-yard trees crouch and shudder in the
sour east, all June they rain canker-worms upon the roof,
and then in autumn choke the eaves with a fall of tattered
and hectic foliage. From the window the fading sisters
gaze upon the unnatural liveliness of the summer streets
through which the summer boarders are driving, or upon
the death-white drifts of the intolerable winter. Their
father, the captain, is dead; he died with the Calcutta
trade, having survived their mother, and left them a
hopeless competency and yonder bamboo chairs; their
only brother is in California; one, though she loved, had
never a lover; her sister's betrothed married West, whither
he went to make a home for her,—and ah! is it vases for
the desolate parlor mantel they decorate, or funeral urns?
And when in time, they being gone, the Californian

brother sends to sell out at auction the old place with the household and kitchen furniture, is it withered rose-leaves or ashes that the purchaser finds in these jars?

They are empty now; and I wonder how came they here? How came the show-case of Dr. Merrifield, Surgeon-Chiropodist here? How came here yon Italian painting?— a poor, silly, little affected Madonna, simpering at me from her dingy gilt frame till I buy her, a great bargain, at a dollar. From what country church or family oratory, in what revolution, or stress of private fortunes,—then from what various cabinets of antiquities, in what dear Vicenza, or Ferrara, or Mantua, earnest thou, O Madonna? Whose likeness are you, poor girl, with your everyday prettiness of brows and chin, and your Raphaelesque crick in the neck? I think I know a part of your story. You were once the property of that ruined advocate, whose sensibilities would sometimes consent that a *valet de place* of uncommon delicacy should bring to his ancestral palace some singularly meritorious foreigner desirous of purchasing from his rare collection,—a collection of rubbish scarcely to be equaled elsewhere in Italy. You hung in that family-room, reached after passage through stately vestibules and grand stairways; and O, I would be cheated to the bone, if only I might look out again from some such windows as were there, upon some such damp, mouldy, broken-statued, ruinous, enchanted garden as lay below! In that room sat the advocate's mother and hunchback sister, with their smoky *scaldini* and their snuffy priest; and there the wife of the foreigner, self-elected the taste of his party, inflicted the pang courted by the advocate, and asked if you were for sale. And then the ruined advocate clasped his hands, rubbed them, set his head heart-brokenly on one side, took you down, heaved a sigh, shrugged his shoulders, and sold you—you! a family heirloom! Well, at least you are old, and you represent to me acres of dim, religious canvas in that beloved land;

and here is the dollar now asked for you: I could not have bought you for so little at home.

The Madonna is neighbored by several paintings, if the kind called Grecian for a reason never revealed by the inventor of an art as old as potichomanie itself. It was an art by which ordinary lithographs were given a ghastly transparency, and a tone as disagreeable as chromos; and I doubt if it could have been known to the Greeks in their best age. But I remember very well when it passed over whole neighborhoods in some parts of this country, wasting the time of many young women, and disfiguring parlor walls with the fruit of their accomplishment. It was always taught by Professors, a class of learned young men who acquired their title by abandoning the plough and anvil, and, in a suit of ready-made clothing, travelling about the country with portfolios under their arms. It was an experience to make loafers for life of them: and I fancy the girls who learnt their art never afterwards made so good butter and cheese.

"Non-ragioniam di lor, ma guarda e passa."

Besides the Grecian paintings there are some mezzotints; full length pictures of presidents and statesmen, chiefly General Jackson, Henry Clay, and Daniel Webster, which have hung their day in the offices or parlors of country politicians. They are all statesmanlike and presidential in attitude; and I know that if the mighty Webster's lips had language, he would take his hand out of his waistcoat front, and say to his fellow mezzotints: "Venerable men! you have come down to us from a former generation, bringing your household furniture and miscellaneous trumpery of all kinds with you."

Some old-fashioned entry lanterns divide my interest with certain old willow chairs of an hour-glass pattern, which never stood upright, probably, and have now all a confirmed droop to one side, as from having been fallen heavily asleep in, upon breezy porches, of hot summer afternoons. In the windows are small vases of alabaster, fly-specked Parian and plaster figures, and dolls with stiff wooden limbs and papier-mache heads, a sort of dolls no longer to be bought in these days of modish, blue-eyed blondes of biscuit and sturdy india-rubber brunettes. The show-case is full of an incredible variety, as photograph albums, fishing-hooks, socks, suspenders, steel pens, cutlery of all sorts, and curious old colored prints of Adelaide, and Kate, and Ellen. A rocking-horse is stabled near amid pendent lengths of second-hand carpeting, hat-racks, and mirrors; and standing cheek-by-jowl with painted washstands and bureaus are some plaster statues, aptly colored and varnished to represent bronze.

There is nothing here but has a marked character of its own, some distinct yet intangible trait acquired from former circumstances; and doubtless all these things have that lurking likeness to former owners which clothes and furniture are apt to take on from long association, and which we should instantly recognize could they be confronted with their late proprietors. It seems, in very imaginative moments, as if the strange assemblage of incongruities must have a consciousness of these latent resemblances, which the individual pieces betray when their present keeper turns the key upon them, and abandons them to themselves at night; and I have sometimes fancied such an effect in the late twilight, when I have wandered into their resting-place, and have beheld them in the unnatural glare of a kerosene lamp burning before a brightly polished reflector, and casting every manner of grotesque shadow upon the floor and walls. But this may have been an illusion; at any rate I am satisfied that the bargain-driving capacity of the store-keeper is not in the least affected by a weird quality in his wares; though they have not failed to impart to him something of their own desultory character. He sometimes leaves a neighbor in charge when he goes to meals, and then, if I enter, I am watchfully followed about from corner to corner, and from room to room, lest I pocket a mattress or slip a book-case under my coat. The store-keeper himself never watches me; perhaps he knows that it is a purely professional interest I take in the collection; that I am in the trade and have a secondhand shop of my own, full of poetical rubbish, and every sort of literary odds and ends, picked up at random, and all cast higgledy-piggledy into the same chaotic receptacle. His customers are as little like ordinary shoppers as he is like common tradesmen. They are in part the Canadians who work in the brickyards, and it is surprising to find how much business can be transacted, and how many sharp bargains struck without the help of a common language. I am in the belief, which may be erroneous, that nobody is wronged in these trades. The taciturn storekeeper, who regards his customers with a stare of solemn amusement as Critturs born by some extraordinary vicissitude of nature to the use of a language that practically amounts to deafness and dumbness, never suffers his philosophical interest in them to affect his commercial efficiency; he drops them now and then a curt English phrase, or expressive Yankee idiom; he knows very well when they mean to buy and when they do not; and they equally wary and equally silent, unswayed by the glib allurements of a salesman, judge of price and quality for themselves, make their solitary offer, and stand or fall by it.

I am seldom able to conclude a pedestrian tour without a glance at the wonderful interior of this cheap store, and I know all its contents familiarly. I recognize wares that have now been on sale there for years; I miss at first glance such accustomed objects as have been parted with between my frequent visits, and hail with pleasure the additions to that extraordinary variety. I can hardly, I suppose, expect the reader to sympathize with the joy I felt the other night, in discovering among the latter an adventurous and universally applicable sign-board advertising This House and Lot for Sale, and, intertwined with the cast-off suspenders which long garlanded a coffee-mill pendent from the roof, a newly added second-hand india-rubber ear-trumpet. Here and there, however, I hope a finer soul will relish, as I do, the poetry of thus buying and offering for sale the very most recondite, as well as the commonest articles of commerce, in the faith that one day the predestined purchaser will appear and carry off the article appointed him from the beginning of time. This faith is all the more touching, because the collector cannot expect to live until the whole stock is disposed of, and because, in the order of nature, much must at last fall to rein unbought, unless the reporter's Devouring Element appears and gives a sudden tragical turn to the poem.

It is the whistle of a train drawing up at the neighboring station that calls me away from the second-hand store; for I never find myself able to resist the hackneyed prodigy of such an arrival. It cannot cease to be impressive. I stand beside the track while the familiar monster writhes up to the station and disgorges its passengers,—suburbanly packaged, and bundled, and bagged, and even when empty-handed somehow proclaiming the jaded character of men that hurry their work all day to catch the evening train out, and their dreams all night to catch the morning train in,—and then I climb the station-stairs, and "hang with grooms and porters on the bridge," that I may not lose my ever-repeated sensation of having the train pass under my feet, and of seeing it rush away westward to the pretty blue hills beyond,—hills not too big for a man born in a plain-country to love. Twisting and trembling along the track, it dwindles rapidly in the perspective, and is presently out of sight. It has left the city and the suburbs behind, and has sought the woods and meadows; but Nature never in the least accepts it, and rarely makes its path a part of her landscape's loveliness. The train passes alien through all her moods and aspects; the wounds made in her face by the road's sharp cuts and excavations are slowest of all wounds to heal, and the iron rails remain to the last as shackles upon her. Yet when the rails are removed, as has happened with a non-paying track in Charlesbridge, the road inspires a real tenderness in her. Then she bids it take or the grace that belongs to all ruin; the grass creeps stealthily over the scarified sides of the embankments; the golden-rod, and the purple-topped iron-weed, and the lady's-slipper, spring up in the hollows on either side, and—I am still thinking of that deserted railroad which runs through Charlesbridge—hide with their leafage the empty tomato-cans and broken bottles and old boots on the ash-heaps dumped there; Nature sets her velvety willows a waving near, and lower than their airy tops plans a vista of trees arching above the track, which is as wild and pretty and illusive a vista as the sunset ever cared to look through and gild a board fence beyond.

Most of our people come from Boston on the horse-cars, and it is only the dwellers on the Avenue and the neighboring streets whom hurrying homeward I follow away from the steam-car station. The Avenue is our handsomest street; and if it were in the cosmopolitan citizen of Charlesbridge to feel any local interest, I should be proud of it. As matters are, I perceive its beauty, and I often reflect, with a pardonable satisfaction, that it is not only handsome, but probably the very dullest street in the world. It is magnificently long and broad, and is flanked nearly the whole way from the station to the colleges by pine palaces rising from spacious lawns, or from the green of trees or the brightness of gardens. The splendor is all very new, but newness is not a fault that much affects architectural beauty, while it is the only one that time is certain to repair: and I find an honest and unceasing pleasure in the graceful lines of those palaces, which is not surpassed even by my appreciation of the vast quiet and monotony of the street itself. Commonly, when I emerge upon it from the grassy-bordered, succory-blossomed walks of Benicia Street, I behold, looking northward, a monumental horse-car standing—it appears for ages, if I wish to take it for Boston—at the head of Pliny Street; and looking southward I see that other emblem of suburban life, an express-wagon, fading rapidly in the distance. Haply the top of a buggy nods round the bend under the elms near the station; and, if fortune is so lavish, a lady appears from a side street, and, while tarrying for the car, thrusts the point of her sun-umbrella into the sandy sidewalk. This is the mid-afternoon effect of the Avenue; but later in the day, and well into the dusk, it remembers its former gayety as a trotting-course,—with here and there a spider-wagon, a twinkling-footed mare, and a guttural driver. On market-days its superb breadth is taken up by flocks of bleating sheep, and a pastoral tone is thus given to its tranquillity; anon a herd of beef-cattle appears under the elms; or a drove of pigs, many pausing, inquisitive of the gutters, and quarrelsome as if they were the heirs of prosperity instead of doom, is slowly urged on toward the shambles. In the spring or the autumn, the Avenue is exceptionally enlivened by the progress of a brace or so of students who, in training for one of the University Courses of base-ball or boating, trot slowly and earnestly along the sidewalk, fists up, elbows down, mouths shut, and a sense of immense responsibility visible in their faces.

The summer is waning with the day as I turn from the Avenue into Benicia Street. This is the hour when the fly cedes to the mosquito, as the Tuscan poet says, and, as one may add, the frying grasshopper yields to the shrilly cricket in noisiness. The embrowning air rings with the sad music made by these innumerable little violinists, hid in all the gardens round, and the pedestrian feels a sinking of the spirits not to be accounted for upon the theory that the street is duller than the Avenue, for it really is not so.

Quick now, the cheerful lamps of kerosene!—without their light, the cry of those crickets, dominated for an instant, but not stilled, by the bellowing of a near-passing locomotive, and the baying of a distant dog, were too much. If it were the last autumn that ever was to be, it could not be heralded with notes of dismaller effect. This is in fact the hour of supreme trial everywhere, and doubtless no one but a newly-accepted lover can be happy at twilight. In the city, even, it is oppressive; in the country it is desolate; in the suburbs it is a miracle that it is ever lived through. The night-winds have not risen yet to stir the languid foliage of the sidewalk maples; the lamps are not yet lighted, to take away the gloom from the blank, staring windows of the houses near; it is too late for letters, too early for a book. In town your fancy would turn to the theatres; in the country you would occupy yourself with cares of poultry or of stock: in the suburbs you can but sit upon your threshold, and fight the predatory mosquito.

BY HORSE-CAR TO BOSTON

At a former period the writer of this had the fortune to serve his country in an Italian city whose great claim upon the world's sentimental interest is the fact that—

"The sea is in her broad, her narrow streets
Ebbing and flowing,"

and that she has no ways whatever for hoofs or wheels. In his quality of United States official, he was naturally called upon for information concerning the estates of Italians believed to have emigrated early in the century to Buenos Ayres, and was commissioned to learn why certain persons in Mexico and Brazil, and the parts of Peru, had not, if they were still living, written home to their friends. On the other hand, he was intrusted with business nearly as pertinent and hopeful by some of his own countrymen, and it was not quite with surprise that he one day received a neatly lithographed circular with his name and address written in it, signed by a famous projector of such enterprises, asking him to cooperate for the introduction of horse-railroads in Venice. The obstacles to the scheme were of such a nature that it seemed hardly worth while even to reply to the circular; but the proposal was one of those bold flights of imagination which forever lift objects out of vulgar association. It has cast an enduring, poetic charm even

W. D. Howells

about the horse-car in my mind, and I naturally look for many unprosaic aspects of humanity there. I have an acquaintance who insists that it is the place above all others suited to see life in every striking phase. He pretends to have witnessed there the reunion of friends who had not met in many years, the embrace, figurative of course, of long lost brothers, the reconciliation of lovers; I do not know but also some scenes of love-making, and acceptance or rejection. But my friend is an imaginative man, and may make himself romances. I myself profess to have beheld for the most part only mysteries; and I think it not the least of these that, riding on the same cars day after day, one finds so many strange faces with so little variety. Whether or not that dull, jarring motion shakes inward and settles about the centres of mental life the sprightliness that should inform the visage, I do not know; but it is certain that the emptiness of the average passenger's countenance is something wonderful, considered with reference to Nature's abhorrence of a vacuum, and the intellectual repute which Boston enjoys among envious New-Yorkers. It is seldom that a journey out of our cold metropolis is enlivened by a mystery so positive in character as the young lady in black, who alighted at a most ordinary little street in Old Charlesbridge, and heightened her effect by going into a French-roof house there that had no more right than a dry goods box to receive a mystery. She was tall, and her lovely arms showed through the black gauze of her dress with an exquisite roundness and *morbidezza*. Upon her beautiful wrists she had heavy bracelets of dead gold, fashioned after some Etruscan device; and from her dainty ears hung great hoops of the same metal and design, which had the singular privilege of touching, now and then, her white columnar neck. A massive chain or necklace, also Etruscan, and also gold, rose and fell at her throat, and on one little ungloved hand glittered a multitude of rings. This hand was very expressive, and took a principal part in the talk which the lady held with her companion, and was as alert and quick as if trained in the gesticulation of Southern or Latin life somewhere. Her features, on the contrary, were rather insipid, being too small and fine; but they were redeemed by the liquid splendor of her beautiful eyes, and the mortal pallor of her complexion. She was altogether so startling an apparition, that all of us jaded, commonplace spectres turned and fastened our weary, lack-lustre eyes upon her looks, with an utter inability to remove them. There was one fat, unctuous person seated opposite, to whom his interest was a torture, for he would have gone to sleep except for her remarkable presence: as it was, his heavy eyelids fell half-way shut, and drooped there at an agonizing angle, while his eyes remained immovably fixed upon that strange, death-white face. How it could have come of that colorlessness,— whether through long sickness or long residence in a tropical climate,—was a question that perplexed another of the passengers, who would have expected to hear the lady speak any language in the world rather than English; and to whom her companion or attendant was hardly less than herself a mystery,—being a dragon-like, elderish female, clearly a Yankee by birth, but apparently of many years' absence from home. The propriety of extracting these people from the horse-cars and transferring them bodily to the first chapter of a romance was a thing about which there could be no manner of doubt, and nothing prevented the abduction but the unexpected voluntary exit of the pale lady. As she passed out everybody else awoke as from a dream, or as if freed from a potent fascination. It is part of the mystery that this lady should never have reappeared in that theatre of life, the horse-car; but I cannot regret having never seen her more; she was so inestimably precious to wonder that it would have been a kind of loss to learn anything about her.

On the other hand, I should be glad if two young men

who once presented themselves as mysteries upon the same stage could be so distinctly and sharply identified that all mankind should recognize them at the day of judgment. They were not so remarkable in the nature as in the degree of their offense; for the mystery that any man should keep his seat in a horse-car and let a woman stand is but too sadly common. They say that this, public unkindness to the sex has come about through the ingratitude of women, who have failed to return thanks for places offered them, and that it is a just and noble revenge we take upon them. There might be something advanced in favor of the idea that we law-making men, who do not oblige the companies to provide seats for every one, deserve no thanks from voteless, helpless women when we offer them places; nay, that we ought to be glad if they do not reproach us for making that a personal favor which ought to be a common right. I would prefer, on the whole, to believe that this selfishness is not a concerted act on our part, but a flower of advanced civilization; it is a ripe fruit in European countries, and it is more noticeable in Boston than anywhere else in America. It is, in fact, one of the points of our high polish which people from the interior say first strikes them on coming among us; for they declare—no doubt too modestly—that in their Boeotian wilds our Athenian habit is almost unknown. Yet it would not be fair to credit our whole population with it. I have seen a laborer or artisan rise from his place, and offer it to a lady, while a dozen well-dressed men kept theirs; and I know several conservative young gentlemen, who are still so old-fashioned as always to respect the weakness and weariness of women. One of them, I hear, has settled it in his own mind that if the family cook appears in a car where he is seated, he must rise and give her his place. This, perhaps, is a trifle idealistic; but it is magnificent, it is princely. From his difficult height, we decline—through ranks that sacrifice themselves for women with bundles or children in arms, for old ladies, or for very young and pretty ones—to the men who give no odds to the most helpless creature alive. These are the men who do not act upon the promptings of human nature like the laborer, and who do not refine upon their duty like my young gentlemen, and make it their privilege to befriend the idea of womanhood; they are men who have paid for their seats and are going to keep them. They have been at work, very probably, all day, and no doubt they are tired; they look so, and try hard not to look ashamed of publicly considering themselves before a sex which is born tired, and from which our climate and customs have drained so much health that society sometimes seems little better than a hospital for invalid woman, where every courtesy is likely to be a mercy done to a sufferer. Yet the two young men of whom I began to speak were not apparently of this class, and let us hope they were foreigners,—say Englishmen, since we hate Englishmen the most. They were the only men seated, in a car full of people; and when four or five ladies came in and occupied the aisle before them, they might have been puzzled which to offer their places to, if one of the ladies had not plainly been infirm. They settled the question—if there was any in their minds—by remaining seated, while the lady in front of them swung uneasily to and fro with the car, and appeared ready to sink at their feet. In another moment she had actually done so; and, too weary to rise, she continued to crouch upon the floor of the car for the course of a mile, the young men resolutely keeping their places, and not rising till they were ready to leave the car. It was a horrible scene, and incredible,—that well-dressed woman sitting on the floor, and those two well-dressed men keeping their places; it was as much out of keeping with our smug respectabilities as a hanging, and was a spectacle so paralyzing that public opinion took no action concerning it. A shabby person, standing upon the platform outside, swore about it, between expectorations:

even the conductor's heart was touched; and he said he had seen a good many hard things aboard horse-cars, but that was a little the hardest; he had never expected to come to that. These were simple people enough, and could not interest me a great deal, but I should have liked to have a glimpse of the complex minds of those young men, and I should still like to know something of the previous life that could have made their behavior possible to them. They ought to make public the philosophic methods by which they reached that pass of unshamable selfishness. The information would be useful to a race which knows the sweetness of self-indulgence, and would fain know the art of so drugging or besotting the sensibilities that it shall no feel disgraced by any sort of meanness. They might really have much to say for themselves; as, that the lady, being conscious she could no longer keep her feet, had no right to crouch at theirs, and put them to so severe a test; or that, having suffered her to sink there, they fell no further in the ignorant public opinion by suffering her to continue there.

But I doubt if that other young man could say anything for himself, who, when a pale, trembling woman was about to drop into the vacant place at his side, stretched his arm across it with, "This seat's engaged," till a robust young fellow, his friend, appeared, and took it and kept it all the way out from Boston. The commission of such a tragical wrong, involving a violation of common usage as well as the infliction of a positive cruelty, would embitter the life of an ordinary man, if any ordinary man were capable of it; but let us trust that nature has provided fortitude of every kind for the offender, and that he is not wrung by keener remorse than most would feel for a petty larceny. I dare say he would be eager at the first opportunity to rebuke the ingratitude of women who do not thank their benefactors for giving them seats. It seems a little odd, by the way, and perhaps it is through the peculiar blessing of Providence, that, since men have determined by a savage egotism to teach the offending sex manners, their own comfort should be in the infliction of the penalty, and that it should be as much a pleasure as a duty to keep one's place.

Perhaps when the ladies come to vote, they will abate, with other nuisances, the whole business of overloaded public conveyances. In the mean time the kindness of women to each other is a notable feature of all horse-car journeys. It is touching to see the smiling eagerness with which the poor things gather close their volumed skirts and make room for a weary sister, the tender looks of compassion which they bend upon the sufferers obliged to stand, the sweetness with which they rise, if they are young and strong, to offer their place to any infirm or heavily burdened person of their sex.

But a journey to Boston is not entirely an experience of bitterness. On the contrary, there are many things besides the mutual amiability of these beautiful martyrs which relieve its tedium and horrors. A whole car-full of people, brought into the closest contact with one another, yet in the absence of introductions never exchanging a word, each being so sufficient to himself as to need no social stimulus whatever, is certainly an impressive and stately spectacle. It is a beautiful day, say; but far be it from me to intimate as much to my neighbor, who plainly would rather die than thus commit himself with me, and who, in fact, would well-nigh strike me speechless with surprise if he did so. If there is any necessity for communication, as with the conductor, we essay first to express ourselves by gesture, and then utter our desires with a certain hollow and remote effect, which is not otherwise to be described. I have sometimes tried to speak above my breath, when, being about to leave the car, I have made a virtue of offering my place to the prettiest young woman standing,

W. D. Howells

but I have found it impossible; the *genius loci*, whatever it was, suppressed me, and I have gasped out my sham politeness as in a courteous nightmare. The silencing influence is quite successfully resisted by none but the tipsy people who occasionally ride out with us, and call up a smile, sad as a gleam of winter sunshine, to our faces by their artless prattle. I remember one eventful afternoon that we were all but moved to laughter by the gayeties of such a one, who, even after he had ceased to talk, continued to amuse us by falling asleep, and reposing himself against the shoulder of the lady next him. Perhaps it is in acknowledgment of the agreeable variety they contribute to horse-car life, that the conductor treats his inebriate passengers with such unfailing tenderness and forbearance. I have never seen them molested, though I have noticed them in the indulgence of many eccentricities, and happened once even to see one of them sit down in a lady's lap. But that was on the night of Saint Patrick's day. Generally all avoidable indecorums are rare in the horse-cars, though during the late forenoon and early afternoon, in the period of lighter travel, I have found curious figures there:—among others, two old women, in the old-clothes business, one of whom was dressed, not very fortunately, in a gown with short sleeves, and inferentially a low neck; a mender of umbrellas, with many unwholesome whity-brown wrecks of umbrellas about him; a peddler of soap, who offered cakes of it to his fellow-passengers at a discount, apparently for friendship's sake; and a certain gentleman with a pock-marked face, and a beard dyed an unscrupulous purple, who sang himself a hymn all the way to Boston, and who gave me no sufficient reason for thinking him a sea-captain. Not far from the end of the Long Bridge, there is apt to be a number of colored ladies waiting to get into the car, or to get out of it,—usually one solemn mother in Ethiopia, and two or three mirthful daughters, who find it hard to suppress a sense of adventure, and to keep in the laughter that struggles out through their glittering teeth and eyes, and who place each other at a disadvantage by divers accidental and intentional bumps and blows. If they are to get out, the old lady is not certain of the place where, and, after making the car stop, and parleying with the conductor, returns to her seat, and is mutely held up to public scorn by one taciturn wink of the conductor's eye.

Among horse-car types, I am almost ashamed to note one so common and observable as that middle-aged lady who gets aboard and will not see the one vacant seat left, but stands tottering at the door, blind and deaf to all the modest beckonings and benevolent gasps of her fellow-passengers. An air as of better days clings about her; she seems a person who has known sickness and sorrow; but so far from pitying her, you view her with inexpressible rancor, for it is plain that she ought to sit down, and that she will not. But for a point of honor the conductor would show her the vacant place; this forbidding, however, how can he? There she stands and sniffs drearily when you glance at her, as you must from time to time, and no wild turkey caught in a trap was ever more incapable of looking down than this middle-aged (shall I say also unmarried?) lady.

Of course every one knows the ladies and gentlemen who sit cater-cornered, and who will not move up; and equally familiar is that large and ponderous person, who, feigning to sit down beside you, practically sits down upon you, and is not incommoded by having your knee under him. He implies by this brutal conduct that you are taking up more space than belongs to you, and that you are justly made an example of.

I had the pleasure one day to meet on the horse-car an advocate of one of the great reforms of the day. He held a

W. D. Howells

green bag upon his knees, and without any notice passed from a question of crops to a discussion of suffrage for the negro, and so to womanhood suffrage. "Let the women vote," said he,—"let 'em vote if they want to. *I* don't care. Fact is, I should like to see 'em do it the first time. They're excitable, you know; they're excitable;" and he enforced his analysis of female character by thrusting his elbow sharply into my side. "Now, there's my wife; I'd like to see her vote. Be fun, I tell you. And the girls,— Lord, the girls! Circus wouldn't be anywhere." Enchanted with the picture which he appeared to have conjured up for himself, he laughed with the utmost relish, and then patting the green bag in his lap, which plainly contained a violin, "You see," he went on, "I go out playing for dancing-parties. Work all day at my trade,—I'm a carpenter,—and play in the evening. Take my little old ten dollars a night. And *I* notice the women a good deal; and *I* tell you they're *all* excitable, and *I sh'd* like to see 'em vote. Vote right and vote often,—that's the ticket, eh?" This friend of womanhood suffrage—whose attitude of curiosity and expectation seemed to me representative of that of a great many thinkers on the subject—no doubt was otherwise a reformer, and held that the coming man would not drink wine—if he could find whiskey. At least I should have said so, guessing from the odors he breathed along with his liberal sentiments.

Something of the character of a college-town is observable nearly always in the presence of the students, who confound certain traditional ideas of students by their quietude of costume and manner, and whom Padua or Heidelberg would hardly know, but who nevertheless betray that they are banded to—

"Scorn delights and live laborious days,"

by a uniformity in the cut of their trousers, or a

clannishness of cane or scarf, or a talk of boats and base-ball held among themselves. One cannot see them without pleasure and kindness; and it is no wonder that their young-lady acquaintances brighten so to recognize them on the horse-cars. There is much good fortune in the world, but none better than being an undergraduate twenty years old, hale, handsome, fashionably dressed, with the whole promise of life before: it's a state of things to disarm even envy. With so much youth forever in her heart, it must be hard for our Charlesbridge to grow old: the generations arise and pass away but in her veins is still this tide of warm blood, century in and century out, so much the same from one age to another that it would be hardy to say it was not still one youthfulness. There is a print of the village as it was a cycle since, showing the oldest of the college buildings and upon the street in front a scholar in his scholar's-cap and gown, giving his arm to a very stylish girl of that period, who is dressed wonderfully like the girl of ours, so that but for the student's antique formality of costume, one might believe that he was handing her out to take the horse-car. There is no horse-car in the picture,—that is the only real difference between then and now in our Charlesbridge, perennially young and gay. Have there not ever been here the same grand ambitions, the same high hopes,—and is not the unbroken succession of youth in these?

As for other life on the horse-car, it shows to little or no effect, as I have said. You can, of course, detect certain classes; as, in the morning the business-men going in, to their counters or their desks, and in the afternoon the shoppers coming out, laden with paper parcels. But I think no one can truly claim to know the regular from the occasional passengers by any greater cheerfulness in the faces of the latter. The horse-car will suffer no such inequality as this, but reduces us all to the same level of melancholy. It would be but a very unworthy kind of art

W. D. Howells

which should seek to describe people by such merely external traits as a habit of carrying baskets or large travelling-bags in the car; and the present muse scorns it, but is not above speaking of the frequent presence of those lovely young girls in which Boston and the suburban towns abound, and who, whether they appear with rolls of music in their hands, or books from the circulating-libraries, or pretty parcels or hand-bags, would brighten even the horse-car if fresh young looks and gay and brilliant costumes could do so much. But they only add perplexity to the anomaly, which was already sufficiently trying with its contrasts of splendor and shabbiness, and such intimate association of velvets and patches as you see in the churches of Catholic countries, but nowhere else in the world except in our "coaches of the sovereign people."

In winter, the journey to or from Boston cannot appear otherwise than very dreary to the fondest imagination. Coming out, nothing can look more arctic and forlorn than the river, double-shrouded in ice and snow, or sadder than the contrast offered to the same prospect in summer. Then all is laughing, and it is a joy in every nerve to ride out over the Long Bridge at high tide, and, looking southward, to see the wide crinkle and glitter of that beautiful expanse of water, which laps on one hand the granite quays of the city, and on the other washes among the reeds and wild grasses of the salt-meadows. A ship coming slowly up the channel, or a dingy tug violently darting athwart it, gives an additional pleasure to the eye, and adds something dreamy or vivid to the beauty of the scene. It is hard to say at what hour of the summer's-day the prospect is loveliest; and I am certainly not going to speak of the sunset as the least of its delights. When this exquisite spectacle is presented, the horse-car passenger, happy to cling with one foot to the rear platform-steps, looks out over the shoulder next him into fairy-land.

Crimson and purple the bay stretches westward till its waves darken into the grassy levels, where, here and there, a hay-rick shows perfectly black against the light. Afar off, southeastward and westward, the uplands wear a tinge of tenderest blue; and in the nearer distance, on the low shores of the river, hover the white plumes of arriving and departing trains. The windows of the stately houses that overlook the water take the sunset from it evanescently, and begin to chill and darken before the crimson burns out of the sky. The windows are, in fact, best after nightfall, when they are brilliantly lighted from within; and when, if it is a dark, warm night, and the briny fragrance comes up strong from the falling tide, the lights reflected far down in the still water, bring a dream, as I have heard travelled Bostonians say, of Venice and her magical effects in the same kind. But for me the beauty of the scene needs the help of no such association; I am content with it for what it is. I enjoy also the hints of spring which one gets in riding over the Long Bridge at low tide in the first open days. Then there is not only a vernal beating of carpets on the piers of the drawbridge, but the piles and walls left bare by the receding water show green patches of sea-weeds and mosses, and flatter the willing eye with a dim hint of summer. This reeking and saturated herbage—which always seems to me, in contrast with dry land growths, what the water-logged life of seafaring folk is to that which we happier men lead on shore,—taking so kindly the deceitful warmth and brightness of the sun, has then a charm which it loses when summer really comes; nor does one, later, have so keen an interest in the men wading about in the shallows below the bridge, who, as in the distance they stoop over to gather whatever shell-fish they seek, make a very fair show of being some ungainlier sort of storks, and are as near as we can hope to come to the spring-prophesying storks of song and story. A sentiment of the drowsiness that goes before the awakening of the year, and is so

W. D. Howells

different from the drowsiness that precedes the great autumnal slumber, is in the air, but is gone when we leave the river behind, and strike into the straggling village beyond.

I maintain that Boston, as one approaches it and passingly takes in the line of Bunker Hill Monument, soaring preeminent among the emulous foundry-chimneys of the sister city, is fine enough to need no comparison with other fine sights. Thanks to the mansard curves and dormer-windows of the newer houses, there is a singularly picturesque variety among the roofs that stretch along the bay, and rise one above another on the city's three hills, grouping themselves about the State House, and surmounted by its India-rubber dome. But, after all, does human weakness crave some legendary charm, some grace of uncertain antiquity, in the picturesqueness it sees? I own that the future, to which we are often referred for the "stuff that dreams are made of," is more difficult for the fancy than the past, that the airy amplitude of its possibilities is somewhat chilly, and that we naturally long for the snug quarters of old, made warm by many generations of life. Besides, Europe spoils us ingenuous Americans, and flatters our sentimentality into ruinous extravagances. Looking at her many-storied former times, we forget our own past, neat, compact, and convenient for the poorest memory to dwell in. Yet an American not infected with the discontent of travel could hardly approach this superb city without feeling something of the coveted pleasure in her, without a reverie of her Puritan and Revolutionary times, and the great names and deeds of her heroic annals. I think, however, we were well to be rid of this yearning for a native American antiquity; for in its indulgence one cannot but regard himself and his contemporaries as cumberers of the ground, delaying the consummation of that hoary past which will be so fascinating to a semi-Chinese posterity, and will be, ages hence, the inspiration of Pigeon-English poetry and romance. Let us make much of our two hundred and fifty years, and cherish the present as our golden age. We healthy-minded people in the horse-cars are loath to lose a moment of it, and are aggrieved that the draw of the bridge should be up, naturally looking on what is constantly liable to happen as an especial malice of the fates. All the drivers of the vehicles that clog the draw on either side have a like sense of personal injury; and apparently it would go hard with the captain of that leisurely vessel below if he were delivered into our hands. But this impatience and anger are entirely illusive.

We are really the most patient people in the world, especially as regards any incorporated, non-political oppressions. A lively Gaul, who travelled among us some thirty years ago, found that, in the absence of political control, we gratified the human instinct of obedience by submitting to small tyrannies unknown abroad, and were subject to the steamboat-captain, the hotel-clerk, the stage-driver, and the waiter, who all bullied us fearlessly; but though some vestiges of this bondage remain, it is probably passing away. The abusive Frenchman's assertion would not at least hold good concerning the horse-car conductors, who, in spite of a lingering prefe- rence for touching or punching passengers for their fare instead of asking for it, are commonly mild-mannered and good-tempered, and disposed to molest us as little as possible. I have even received from one of them a mark of such kindly familiarity as the offer of a check which he held between his lips, and thrust out his face to give me, both his hands being otherwise occupied; and their lives are in nowise such luxurious careers as we should expect in public despots. The oppression of the horse-car passenger is not from them, and the passenger himself is finally to blame for it. When the draw closes at last, and we rumble forward into the city street, a certain stir of

W. D. Howells

expectation is felt among us. The long and eventful journey is nearly ended, and now we who are to get out of the cars can philosophically amuse ourselves with the passions and sufferings of those who are to return in our places. You must choose the time between five and six o'clock in the afternoon, if you would make this grand study of the national character in its perfection. Then the spectacle offered in any arriving horse-car will serve your purpose. At nearly every corner of the street up which it climbs stands an experienced suburban, who darts out upon the car, and seizes a vacant place in it. Presently all the places are taken, and before we reach Temple Street, where helpless groups of women are gathered to avail themselves of the first seats vacated, an alert citizen is stationed before each passenger who is to retire at the summons, "Please pass out forrad." When this is heard in Bowdoin Square, we rise and push forward, knuckling one another's backs in our eagerness, and perhaps glancing behind us at the tumult within. Not only are all our places occupied, but the aisle is left full of passengers precariously supporting themselves by the straps in the roof. The rear platform is stormed and carried by a party with bundles; the driver is instantly surrounded by another detachment; and as the car moves away from the office, the platform steps are filled.

"Is it possible," I asked myself, when I had written as far as this in the present noble history, "that I am not exaggerating? It can't be that this and the other enormities I have been describing are of daily occurrence in Boston. Let me go verify, at least, my picture of the evening horse-car." So I take my way to Bowdoin Square, and in the conscientious spirit of modern inquiry, I get aboard the first car that comes up. Like every other car, it is meant to seat twenty passengers. It does this, and besides it carries in the aisle and on the platform forty passengers standing. The air is what you may imagine, if you know that not only is the place so indecently crowded, but that in the centre of the car are two adopted citizens, far gone in drink, who have the aspect and the smell of having passed the day in an ash-heap. These citizens being quite helpless themselves, are supported by the public, and repose in singular comfort upon all the passengers near them; I, myself, contribute an aching back to the common charity, and a genteelly dressed young lady takes one of them from time to time on her knee. But they are comparatively an ornament to society till the conductor objects to the amount they offer him for fare; for after that they wish to fight him during the journey, and invite him at short intervals to step out and be shown what manner of men they are. The conductor passes it off for a joke, and so it is, and a very good one.

In that unhappy mass it would be an audacious spirit who should say of any particular arm or leg, "It is mine," and all the breath is in common. Nothing, it would seem, could add to our misery; but we discover our error when the conductor squeezes a tortuous path through us, and collects the money for our transportation. I never can tell, during the performance of this feat, whether he or the passengers are more to be pitied.

The people who are thus indecorously huddled and jammed together, without regard to age or sex, otherwise lead lives of at least comfort, and a good half of them cherish themselves in every physical way with unparalleled zeal. They are handsomely clothed; they are delicately neat in linen; they eat well, or, if not well, as well as their cooks will let them, and at all events expensively; they house in dwellings appointed in a manner undreamt of elsewhere in the world,—dwellings wherein furnaces make a summer-heat, where fountains of hot and cold water flow at a touch, where light is created or quenched by the turning of a key, where all is luxurious upholstery, and magical ministry to real or fancied needs. They carry the same tastes with them to their places of business; and when they "attend divine service," it is with the understanding that God is to receive them in a richly carpeted house, deliciously warmed and perfectly ventilated, where they may adore Him at their ease upon cushioned seats,—secured seats. Yet these spoiled children of comfort, when they ride to or from business or church, fail to assert rights that the benighted Cockney, who never heard of our plumbing and registers, or even the oppressed Parisian, who is believed not to change his linen from one revolution to another, having paid for, enjoys. When they enter the "full" horse-car, they find themselves in a place inexorable as the grave to their greenbacks, where not only is their adventitious consequence stripped from them, but the courtesies of life are impossible, the inherent dignity of the person is denied, and they are reduced below the level of the most uncomfortable nations of the Old World. The philosopher accustomed to draw consolation from the sufferings of his richer fellow-men, and to infer an overruling Providence from their disgraces, might well bless Heaven for the spectacle of such degradation, if his thanksgiving were not prevented by his knowledge that this is quite voluntary. And now consider that on every car leaving the city at this time the scene is much the same; reflect that the horror is enacting, not only in Boston, but in New York, Philadelphia, Baltimore, St. Louis, Chicago, Cincinnati,—wherever the horse-car, that tinkles well-nigh round the Continent, is known; remember that the same victims are thus daily sacrificed, without an effort to right themselves: and then you will begin to realize— dimly and imperfectly, of course—the unfathomable meekness of the American character. The "full" horse-car is a prodigy whose likeness is absolutely unknown elsewhere, since the Neapolitan gig went out; and I suppose it will be incredible to the future in our own country. When I see such a horse-car as I have sketched move away from its station, I feel that it is something not only emblematic and interpretative, but monumental; and I know that when art becomes truly national, the overloaded horse-car will be celebrated in painting and sculpture. And in after ages, when the oblique-eyed, swarthy American of that time, pausing before some commemorative bronze or historical picture of our epoch, contemplates this stupendous spectacle of human endurance, I hope he will be able to philosophize more satisfactorily than we can now, concerning the mystery of our strength as a nation and our weakness as a public.

A DAY'S PLEASURE

I—THE MORNING

They were not a large family, and their pursuits and habits were very simple; yet the summer was lapsing toward the first pathos of autumn before they found themselves all in such case as to be able to take the day's pleasure they had planned so long. They had agreed often and often that nothing could be more charming than an excursion down the Harbor, either to Gloucester, or to Nahant, or to Nantasket Beach, or to Hull and Hingham, or to any point within the fatal bound beyond which is seasickness. They had studied the steamboat advertisements, day after day, for a long time, without making up their minds which of these charming excursions would be the most delightful; and when they had at last fixed upon one and chosen some day for it, that day was sure to be heralded by a long train of obstacles, or it dawned upon weather that was simply impossible. Besides, in the suburbs, you are apt to sleep late, unless the solitary ice-wagon of the neighborhood makes a very uncommon rumbling in going by; and I believe that the excursion was several times postponed by the tardy return of the pleasurers from dreamland, which, after all, is not the worst resort, or the least interesting—or profitable, for the matter of that. But at last the great day came,—a blameless Thursday alike removed from the cares of washing and ironing days, and from the fatigues with which every week closes. One of the family chose deliberately to stay at home; but the severest scrutiny could not detect a hindrance in the health or circumstances of any of the rest, and the weather was delicious. Everything, in fact, was so fair and so full of promise, that they could almost fancy a calamity of some sort hanging over its perfection, and possibly bred of it; for I suppose that we never have anything made perfectly easy for us without a certain reluctance and foreboding. That morning they all got up so early that they had time to waste over breakfast before taking the 7.30 train for Boston; and they naturally wasted so much of it that they reached the station only in season for the 8.00. But there is a difference between reaching the station and quietly taking the cars, especially if one of your company has been left at home, hoping to cut across and take the cars at a station which they reach some minutes later, and you, the head of the party, are obliged, at a loss of breath and personal comfort and dignity, to run down to that station and see that the belated member has arrived there, and then hurry back to your own, and embody the rest, with their accompanying hand-bags and wraps and sun-umbrellas, into some compact shape for removal into the cars, during the very scant minute that the train stops at Charlesbridge. Then when you are all aboard, and the tardy member has been duly taken up at the next station, and you would be glad to spend the time in looking about on the familiar variety of life which every car presents in every train on every road in this vast American world, you are oppressed and distracted by the cares which must attend the pleasure-seeker, and which the more thickly beset him the more deeply he plunges into enjoyment.

I can learn very little from the note-book of the friend whose adventures I am relating in regard to the scenery of

Somerville, and the region generally through which the railroad passes between Charlesbridge and Boston; but so much knowledge of it may be safely assumed on the part of the reader as to relieve me of the grave responsibility of describing it. Still, I may say that it is not unpicturesque, and that I have a pleasure, which I hope the reader shares, in anything like salt meadows and all spaces subject to the tide, whether flooded by it or left bare with their saturated grasses by its going down. I think, also, there is something fine in the many-roofed, many-chimneyed highlands of Chelsea (if it is Chelsea), as you draw near the railroad bridge, and there is a pretty stone church on a hill-side there which has the good fortune, so rare with modern architecture and so common with the old, of seeming a natural outgrowth of the spot where it stands, and which is as purely an object of aesthetic interest to me, who know nothing of its sect or doctrine, as any church in a picture could be; and there is, also, the Marine Hospital on the heights (if it is the Marine Hospital), from which I hope the inmates can behold the ocean, and exult in whatever misery keeps them ashore.

But let me not so hasten over this part of my friend's journey as to omit all mention of the amphibious Irish houses which stand about on the low lands along the railroad-sides, and which you half expect to see plunge into the tidal mud of the neighborhood, with a series of hoarse croaks, as the train approaches. Perhaps twenty-four trains pass those houses every twenty-four hours, and it is a wonder that the inhabitants keep their interest in them, or have leisure to bestow upon any of them. Yet, as you dash along so bravely, you can see that you arrest the occupations of all these villagers as by a kind of enchantment; the children pause and turn their heads toward you from their mud-pies (to the production of which there is literally no limit in that region); the matron rests one parboiled hand on her hip, letting the other still linger listlessly upon the wash-board, while she lifts her eyes from the suds to look at you; the boys, who all summer long are forever just going into the water or just coming out of it, cease their buttoning or unbuttoning; the baby, which has been run after and caught and suitably posed, turns its anguished eyes upon you, where also falls the mother's gaze, while her descending palm is arrested in mid air. I forbear to comment upon the surprising populousness of these villages, where, in obedience to all the laws of health, the inhabitants ought to be wasting miserably away, but where they flourish in spite of them. Even Accident here seems to be robbed of half her malevolence; and that baby (who will presently be chastised with terrific uproar) passes an infancy of intrepid enjoyment amidst the local perils, and is no more affected by the engines and the cars than by so many fretful hens with their attendant broods of chickens.

When sometimes I long for the excitement and variety of travel, which, for no merit of mine, I knew in other days, I reproach myself, and silence all my repinings with some such question as, Where could you find more variety or greater excitement than abounds in and near the Fitchburg Depot when a train arrives? And to tell the truth, there is something very inspiring in the fine eagerness with which all the passengers rise as soon as the locomotive begins to slow, and huddle forward to the door, in their impatience to get out; while the suppressed vehemence of the hackmen is also thrilling in its way, not to mention the instant clamor of the baggage-men as they read and repeat the numbers of the checks in strident tones. It would be ever so interesting to depict all these people, but it would require volumes for the work, and I reluctantly let them all pass out without a word,—all but that sweet young blonde who arrives by most trains, and who, putting up her eye-glass with a ravishing air, bewitchingly peers round among the bearded faces, with little tender looks of hope and trepidation, for the face which she wants, and which presently bursts through the circle of strange visages. The owner of the face then hurries forward to meet that sweet blonde, who gives him a little drooping hand as if it were a delicate flower she laid in his; there is a brief mutual hesitation long enough merely for an electrical thrill to run from heart to heart through the clasping hands, and then he stoops toward her, and distractingly kisses her. And I say that there is no law of conscience or propriety worthy the name of law— barbarity, absurdity, call it rather—to prevent any one from availing himself of that providential near-sighted-ness, and beatifying himself upon those lips,—nothing to prevent it but that young fellow, whom one might not, of course, care to provoke.

Among the people who now rush forward and heap themselves into the two horse-cars and one omnibus, placed before the depot by a wise forethought for the public comfort to accommodate the train-load of two hundred passengers, I always note a type that is both pleasing and interesting to me. It is a lady just passing middle life; from her kindly eyes the envious crow, whose footprints are just traceable at their corners, has not yet drunk the brightness, but she looks just a thought sadly, if very serenely, from them. I know nothing in the world of her; I may have seen her twice or a hundred times, but I must always be making bits of romances about her. That is she in faultless gray, with the neat leather bag in her lap, and a bouquet of the first autumnal blooms perched in her shapely hands which are prettily yet substantially gloved in some sort of gauntlets. She can be easy and dignified, my dear middle-aged heroine, even in one of our horse-cars, where people are for the most part packed like cattle in a pen. She shows no trace of dust or fatigue from the thirty or forty miles which I choose to fancy she has ridden from the handsome elm-shaded New England town of five or ten thousand people, where I choose to think she lives. From a vague horticultural association with those gauntlets, as well as from the autumnal blooms, I take it she loves flowers, and gardens a good deal with her own hands, and keeps house-plants in the winter, and of course a canary. Her dress, neither rich nor vulgar, makes me believe her fortunes modest and not recent; her gentle face has just so much intellectual character as it is good to see in a woman's face; I suspect that she reads pretty regularly the new poems and histories, and I know that she is the life and soul of the local book-club. Is she married, or widowed, or one of the superfluous forty thousand? That is what I never can tell. But I think that most probably she is married, and that her husband is very much in business, and does not share so much as he respects her tastes. I have no particular reason for thinking that she has no children now, and that the sorrow for the one she lost so long ago has become only a pensive silence, which, however, a long summer twilight can yet deepen to tears.... Upon my word! Am I then one to give way to this sort of thing? Madam, I ask pardon. I have no right to be sentimentalizing you. Yet your face is one to make people dream kind things of you, and I cannot keep my reveries away from it.

But in the mean time I neglect the momentous history which I have proposed to write, and leave my day's pleasurers to fade into the background of a fantastic portrait. The truth is, I cannot look without pain upon the discomforts which they suffer at this stage of their joyous enterprise. At the best, the portables of such a party are apt to be grievous embarrassments: a package of shawls and parasols and umbrellas and India-rubbers, however neatly made up at first, quickly degenerates into a shapeless mass, which has finally to be carried with as great tenderness as an ailing child; and the lunch is pretty sure to overflow the hand-bags and to eddy about you in paper parcels; while the bottle of claret, that bulges the side of one of the bags, and

"That will show itself without,"

defying your attempts to look as it were cold tea, gives a crushing touch of disreputability to the whole affair. Add to this the fact that but half the party have seats, and that the others have to sway and totter about the car in that sudden contact with all varieties of fellow-men, to which we are accustomed in the cars, and you must allow that these poor merrymakers have reasons enough to rejoice when this part of their day's pleasure is over. They are so plainly bent upon a sail down the Harbor, that before they leave the car they become objects of public interest, and are at last made to give some account of themselves.

"Going for a sail, I presume?" says a person hitherto in conversation with the conductor. "Well, I wouldn't mind a sail myself to-day."

"Yes," answers the head of the party, "going to Gloucester."

"Guess not," says, very coldly and decidedly, one of the passengers, who is reading that morning's "Advertiser;" and when the subject of this surmise looks at him for explanations, he adds, "The City Council has chartered the boat for to-day."

Upon this the excursionists fall into great dismay and bitterness, and upbraid the City Council, and wonder why last night's "Transcript" said nothing about its oppressive action, and generally bewail their fate. But at last they resolve to go somewhere, and, being set down, they make up their warring minds upon Nahant, for the Nahant boat leaves the wharf nearest them; and so they hurry away to India Wharf, amidst barrels and bales and boxes and hacks and trucks, with interminable string-teams passing before them at every crossing.

"At any rate," says the leader of the expedition, "we shall see the Gardens of Maolis,—those enchanted gardens which have fairly been advertised into my dreams, and where I've been told," he continues, with an effort to make the prospect an attractive one, yet not without a sense of the meagreness of the materials, "they have a grotto and a wooden bull."

Of course, there is no reason in nature why a wooden bull should be more pleasing than a flesh-and-blood bull, but it seems to encourage the company, and they set off again with renewed speed, and at last reach India Wharf in time to see the Nahant steamer packed full of excursionists, with a crowd of people still waiting to go aboard. It does not look inviting, and they hesitate. In a minute or two their spirits sink so low, that if they should see the wooden bull step out of a grotto on the deck of the steamer the spectacle could not revive them. At that instant they think, with a surprising singleness, of Nantasket Beach, and the bright colors in which the Gardens of Maolis but now appeared fade away, and they seem to see themselves sauntering along the beautiful shore, while the white-crested breakers crash upon the sand, and run up

"In tender-curving lines of creamy spray,"

quite to the feet of that lotus-eating party.

"Nahant is all rocks," says the leader to Aunt Melissa, who hears him with a sweet and tranquil patience, and who would enjoy or suffer anything with the same expression; "and as you've never yet seen the open sea, it's fortunate that we go to Nantasket, for, of course, a beach is more characteristic. But now the object is to get there. The boat will be starting in a few moments, and I doubt whether we can walk it. How far is it," he asks, turning toward a respectable-looking man, "to Liverpool Wharf?"

"Well, it's consid'able ways," says the man, smiling.

"Then we must take a hack," says the pleasurer to his party. "Come on."

"I've got a hack," observes the man, in a casual way, as if the fact might possibly interest.

"O, you have, have you? Well, then, put us into it, and drive to Liverpool Wharf; and hurry."

Either the distance was less than the hackman fancied, or else he drove thither with unheard-of speed, for two minutes later he set them down on Liverpool Wharf. But swiftly as they had come the steamer had been even more prompt, and she now turned toward them a beautiful wake, as she pushed farther and farther out into the harbor.

The hackman took his two dollars for his four passengers, and was rapidly mounting his box,—probably to avoid idle reproaches. "Wait!" said the chief pleasurer. Then, "When does the next boat leave?" he asked of the agent, who had emerged with a compassionate face from the waiting-rooms on the wharf.

"At half past two."

"And it's now five minutes past nine," moaned

the merrymakers.

"Why, I'll tell you what you can do," said the agent; "you can go to Hingham by the Old Colony cars, and so come back by the Hull and Hingham boat."

"That's it!" chorused his listeners, "we'll go;" and "Now," said their spokesman to the driver, "I dare say you didn't know that Liverpool Wharf was so near; but I don't think you've earned your money, and you ought to take us on to the Old Colony Depot for half-fares at the most."

The driver looked pained, as if some small tatters and shreds of conscience were flapping uncomfortably about his otherwise dismantled spirit. Then he seemed to think of his wife and family, for he put on the air of a man who had already made great sacrifices, and "I couldn't, really, I couldn't afford it," said he; and as the victims turned from him in disgust, he chirruped to his horses and drove off.

"Well," said the pleasurers, "we won't give it up. We will have our day's pleasure after all. But what *can* we do to kill five hours and a half? It's miles away from every-thing, and, besides, there's nothing even if we were there." At this image of their remoteness and the inherent desolation of Boston they could not suppress some sighs, and in the mean time Aunt Melissa stepped into the waiting-room, which opened on the farther side upon the water, and sat contentedly down on one of the benches; the rest, from sheer vacuity and irresolution, followed, and thus, without debate, it was settled that they should wait there till the boat left. The agent, who was a kind man, did what he could to alleviate the situation: he gave them each the advertisement of his line of boats, neatly printed upon a card, and then he went away.

All this prospect of waiting would do well enough for the

ladies of the party, but there is an impatience in the masculine fibre which does not brook the notion of such prolonged repose; and the leader of the excursion presently pretended an important errand up town,— nothing less, in fact, than to buy a tumbler out of which to drink their claret on the beach. A holiday is never like any other day to the man who takes it, and a festive halo seemed to enwrap the excursionist as he pushed on through the busy streets in the cool shadow of the vast granite palaces wherein the genius of business loves to house itself in this money-making land, and inhaled the odors of great heaps of leather and spices and dry goods as he passed the open doorways,—odors that mixed pleasantly with the smell of the freshly watered streets. When he stepped into a crockery store to make his purchase a sense of pleasure-taking did not fail him, and he fell naturally into talk with the clerk about the weather and such pastoral topics. Even when he reached the establishment where his own business days were passed some glamour seemed to be cast upon familiar objects. To the disenchanted eye all things were as they were on all other dullish days of summer, even to the accustomed bore leaning up against his favorite desk and transfixing his habitual victim with his usual theme. Yet to the gaze of this pleasure-taker all was subtly changed, and he shook hands right and left as he entered, to the marked surprise of the objects of his effusion. He had merely come to get some newspapers to help pass away the long moments on the wharf, and when he had found these, he hurried back thither to hear what had happened during his absence.

It seemed that there had hardly ever been such an eventful period in the lives of the family before, and he listened to a minute account of it from Cousin Lucy. "You know, Frank," says she, "that Sallie's one idea in life is to keep the baby from getting the whooping-cough, and I declare that these premises have done nothing but reecho with the most dolorous whoops ever since you've been gone, so that at times, in my fear that Sallie would think I'd been careless about the boy, I've been ready to throw myself into the water, and nothing's prevented me but the doubt whether it wouldn't be better to throw in the whoopers instead."

At this moment a pale little girl, with a face wan and sad through all its dirt, came and stood in the doorway nearest the baby, and in another instant she had burst into a whoop so terrific that, if she had meant to have his scalp next it could not have been more dreadful. Then she subsided into a deep and pathetic quiet, with that air peculiar to the victims of her disorder of having done nothing noticeable. But her outburst had set at work the mysterious machinery of half a dozen other whooping-coughers lurking about the building, and all unseen they wound themselves up with appalling rapidity, and in the utter silence which followed left one to think they had died at the climax.

"Why, it's a perfect whooping-cough factory, this place," cries Cousin Lucy in a desperation. "Go away, do, please, from the baby, you poor little dreadful object you," she continues, turning upon the only visible operative in the establishment. "Here, take this," and she bribes her with a bit of sponge-cake, on which the child runs lightly off along the edge of the wharf. "That's been another of their projects for driving me wild," says Cousin Lucy,—"trying to take their own lives in a hundred ways before my face and eyes. Why *will* their mothers let them come here to play?"

Really, they were very melancholy little figures, and might have gone near to make one sad, even if they had not been constantly imperilling their lives. Thanks to its being summer-time, it did not much matter about the scantiness of their clothing, but their squalor was depressing, it seemed, even to themselves, for they were a mournful-looking set of children, and in their dangerous sports trifled silently and almost gloomily with death. There were none of them above eight or nine years of age, and most of them had the care of smaller brothers, or even babes in arms, whom they were thus early inuring to the perils of the situation. The boys were dressed in panta-loons and shirts which no excess of rolling up in the legs and arms could make small enough, and the incorrigible too-bigness of which rendered the favorite amusements still more hazardous from their liability to trip and entangle the wearers. The little girls had on each a solitary garment, which hung about her gaunt person with antique severity of outline; while the babies were multitudinously swathed in whatever fragments of dress could be tied or pinned or plastered on. Their faces were strikingly and almost ingeniously dirty, and their distractions among the coal-heaps and cord-wood constantly added to the variety and advantage of these effects.

"Why do their mothers let them come here?" muses Frank aloud. "Why, because it's so safe, Cousin Lucy. At home, you know, they'd have to be playing upon the sills of fourth-floor windows, and here they're out of the way and can't hurt themselves. Why, Cousin Lucy, this is their park,—their Public Garden, their Bois de Boulogne, their Cascine. And look at their gloomy little faces! Aren't they taking their pleasure in the spirit of the very highest fashion? I was at Newport last summer, and saw the famous driving on the Avenue in those pony phaetons, dog-carts, and tubs, and three-story carriages with a pair of footmen perching like storks upon each gable, and I assure you that all those ornate and costly phantasms (it seems to me now like a sad, sweet vision) had just the expression of these poor children. We're taking a day's pleasure ourselves, cousin, but nobody would know it from our looks. And has nothing but whooping-cough happened since I've been gone?"

"Yes, we seem to be so cut off from every-day associations that I've imagined myself a sort of tourist, and I've been to that Catholic church over yonder, in hopes of seeing the Murillos and Raphaels—but I found it locked up, and so I trudged back without a sight of the masterpieces. But what's the reason that all the shops hereabouts have nothing but luxuries for sale? The windows are perfect tropics of oranges, and lemons, and belated bananas, and tobacco, and peanuts."

"Well, the poor really seem to use more of those luxuries than anybody else. I don't blame them. I shouldn't care for the necessaries of life myself, if I found them so hard to get."

"When I came back here," says Cousin Lucy, without heeding these flippant and heartless words, "I found an old gentleman who has something to do with the boats, and he sat down, as if it were a part of his business, and told me nearly the whole history of his life. Isn't it nice of them, keeping an Autobiographer? It makes the time pass so swiftly when you're waiting. This old gentleman was born—who'd ever think it?—up there in Pearl Street, where those pitiless big granite stores are now; and, I don't know why, but the idea of any human baby being born in Pearl Street seemed to me one of the saddest things I'd ever heard of."

Here Cousin Lucy went to the rescue of the nurse and the baby, who had got into one of their periodical difficulties, and her interlocutor turned to Aunt Melissa.

"I think, Franklin," says Aunt Melissa, "that it was wrong

to let that nurse come and bring the baby."

"Yes, I know, Aunty, you have those old-established ideas, and they're very right," answers her nephew; "but just consider how much she enjoys it, and how vastly the baby adds to the pleasure of this charming excursion!"

Aunt Melissa made no reply, but sat thoughtfully out upon the bay. "I presume you think the excursion is a failure," she said, after a while; "but I've been enjoying every minute of the time here. Of course, I've never seen the open sea, and I don't know about it, but I feel here just as if I were spending a day at the seaside."

"Well," said her nephew, "I shouldn't call this exactly a watering-place. It lacks the splendor and gayety of Newport, in a certain degree, and it hasn't the illustrious seclusion of Nahant. The surf isn't very fine, nor the beach particularly adapted to bathing; and yet, I must confess, the outlook from here is as lovely as anything one need have."

And to tell the truth, it was very pretty and interesting. The landward environment was as commonplace and mean as it could be: a yardful of dismal sheds for coal and lumber, and shanties for offices, with each office its safe and its desk, its whittled arm-chair and its spittoon, its fly that shooed not, but buzzed desperately against the grimy pane, which, if it had really had that boasted microscopic eye, it never would have mistaken for the unblemished daylight. Outside of this yard was the usual wharfish neighborhood, with its turmoil of trucks and carts and fleet express-wagons, its building up and pulling down, its discomfort and clamor of every sort, and its shops for the sale, not only of those luxuries which Lucy had mentioned, but of such domestic refreshments as lemon-pie and hulled-corn.

When, however, you turned your thoughts and eyes away from this aspect of it, and looked out upon the water, the neighborhood gloriously retrieved itself. There its poverty and vulgarity ceased; there its beauty and grace abounded. A light breeze ruffled the face of the bay, and the innumerable little sail-boats that dotted it took the sun and wind upon their wings, which they dipped almost into the sparkle of the water, and flew lightly hither and thither like gulls that loved the brine too well to rise wholly from it; larger ships, farther or nearer, puffed or shrank their sails as they came and went on the errands of commerce, but always moved as if bent upon some dreamy affair of pleasure; the steamboats that shot vehemently across their tranquil courses seemed only gayer and vivider visions, but not more substantial; yonder, a black sea-going steamer passed out between the far-off islands, and at last left in the sky above those reveries of fortification, a whiff of sombre smoke, dark and unreal as a memory of battle; to the right, on some line of railroad, long-plumed trains arrived and departed like pictures passed through the slide of a magic-lantern; even a pile-driver, at work in the same direction, seemed to have no malice in the blows which, after a loud clucking, it dealt the pile, and one understood that it was mere conventional violence like that of a Punch to his baby.

"Why, what a lotus-eating life this is!" said Frank, at last. "Aunt Melissa, I don't wonder you think it's like the seaside. It's a great deal better than the seaside. And now, just as we've entered into the spirit of it, the time's up for the 'Rose Standish' to come and bear us from its delights. When will the boat be in?" he asked of the Autobiographer, whom Lucy had pointed out to him.

"Well, she's *ben* in half an hour, now. There she lays, just outside the 'John Romer.'"

W. D. Howells

There, to be sure, she lay, and those pleasure-takers had been so lost in the rapture of waiting and the beauty of the scene as never to have noticed her arrival.

II—THE AFTERNOON

It is noticeable how many people there are in the world
that seem bent always upon the same purpose of amusement or business as one's self. If you keep quietly about
your accustomed affairs, there are all your neighbors and
acquaintance hard at it too; if you go on a journey, choose
what train you will, the cars are filled with travellers in
your direction. You take a day's pleasure, and everybody
abandons his usual occupation to crowd upon your boat,
whether it is to Gloucester, or Nahant, or to Nantasket
Beach you go. It is very hard to believe that, from
whatever channel of life you abstract yourself, still the
great sum of it presses forward as before: that business is
carried on though you are idle, that men amuse themselves though you toil, that every train is as crowded as
that you travel on, that the theatre or the church fills its
boxes or pews without you perfectly well. I suppose it
would not be quite agreeable to believe all this; the
opposite illusion is far more flattering; for if each one of
us did not take the world with him now at every turn,
should he not have to leave it behind him when he died?
And that, it must be owned, would not be agreeable, nor is
the fact quite conceivable, though ever so many myriads
in so many million years have proved it.

When our friends first went aboard the "Rose Standish"
that day they were almost the sole passengers, and they
had a feeling of ownership and privacy which was
pleasant enough in its way, but which they lost afterwards; though to lose it was also pleasant, for enjoyment
no more likes to be solitary than sin does, which is
notoriously gregarious, and I dare say would hardly exist
if it could not be committed in company. The preacher,
indeed, little knows the comfortable sensation we have in
being called fellow-sinners, and what an effective shield

for his guilt each makes of his neighbor's hard-heartedness.

Cousin Frank never felt how strange was a lonely transgression till that day, when in the silence of the little cabin he took the bottle of claret from the handbag, and prepared to moisten the family lunch with it. "I think, Aunt Melissa," he said, "we had better lunch now, for it's a quarter past two, and we shall not get to the beach before four. Let's improvise a beach of these chairs, and that water-urn yonder can stand for the breakers. Now, this is truly like Newport and Nahant," he added, after the little arrangement was complete; and he was about to strip away the bottle's jacket of brown paper, when a lady much wrapped up came in, and, reclining upon one of the opposite seats, began to take them all in with a severe serenity of gaze that made them feel for a moment like a party of low foreigners,—like a set of German atheists, say. Frank kept on the bottle's paper jacket, and as the single tumbler of the party circled from mouth to mouth, each of them tried to give the honest drink the false air of a medicinal potion of some sort; and to see Aunt Melissa sipping it, no one could have put his hand on his heart and sworn it was not elderberry wine, at the worst. In spite of these efforts, they all knew that they had suffered a hopeless loss of repute; yet after the loss was confessed, I am not sure that they were not the gayer and happier through this "freedom of a broken law." At any rate, the lunch passed off very merrily, and when they had put back the fragments of the feast into the bags, they went forward to the bow of the boat, to get good places for seeing the various people as they came aboard, and for an outlook upon the bay when the boat should start.

I suppose that these were not very remarkable people, and that nothing but the indomitable interest our friends took in the human race could have enabled them to feel any concern in their companions. It was, no doubt, just such a company as goes down to Nantasket Beach every pleasant day in summer. Certain ones among them were distinguishable as sojourners at the beach, by an air of familiarity with the business of getting there, an indifference to the prospect, and an indefinable touch of superiority. These read their newspapers in quiet corners, or, if they were not of the newspaper sex, made themselves comfortable in the cabins, and looked about them at the other passengers with looks of lazy surprise, and just a hint of scorn for their interest in the boat's departure. Our day's pleasurers took it that the lady whose steady gaze had reduced them, when at lunch, to such a low ebb of shabbiness, was a regular boarder, at the least, in one of the beach hotels. A few other passengers were, like themselves, mere idlers for a day, and were eager to see all that the boat or the voyage offered of novelty. There were clerks and men who had book-keeping written in a neat mercantile hand upon their faces, and who had evidently been given that afternoon for a breathing-time; and there were strangers who were going down to the beach for the sake of the charming view of the harbor which the trip afforded. Here and there were people who were not to be classed with any certainty,—as a pale young man, handsome in his undesirable way, who looked like a steamboat pantry boy not yet risen to be bar-tender, but rapidly rising, and who sat carefully balanced upon the railing of the boat, chatting with two young girls, who heard his broad sallies with continual snickers, and interchanged saucy comments with that prompt up-and-coming manner which is so large a part of non-humorous humor, as Mr. Lowell calls it, and now and then pulled and pushed each other. It was a scene worth study, for in no other country could anything so bad have been without being vastly worse; but here it was evident that there was nothing worse than you saw; and, indeed, these persons formed a sort of relief to the other passengers, who were nearly all monotonously well-behaved. Amongst a few there seemed to be acquaintance, but the far greater part were unknown to one another, and there were no words wasted by any one. I believe the English traveller who has taxed our nation with inquisitiveness for half a century is at last beginning to find out that we do not ask questions because we have the still more vicious custom of not opening our mouths at all when with strangers.

It was a good hour after our friends got aboard before the boat left her moorings, and then it was not without some secret dreads of sea-sickness that Aunt Melissa saw the seething brine widen between her and the familiar wharf-house, where she now seemed to have spent so large a part of her life. But the multitude of really charming and interesting objects that presently fell under her eye soon distracted her from those gloomy thoughts.

There is always a shabbiness about the wharves of seaports; but I must own that as soon as you get a reasonable distance from them in Boston, they turn wholly beautiful. They no longer present that imposing array of mighty ships which they could show in the days of Consul Plancus, when the commerce of the world sought chiefly our port, yet the docks are still filled with the modester kinds of shipping, and if there is not that wilderness of spars and rigging which you see at New York, let us believe that there is an aspect of selection and refinement in the scene, so that one should describe it, not as a forest, but, less conventionally, as a gentleman's park of masts. The steamships of many coastwise freight lines gloom, with their black, capacious hulks, among the lighter sailing-craft, and among the white, green-shuttered passenger-boats; and behind them those desperate and grimy sheds assume a picturesqueness, their sagging roofs and crooked gables harmonizing agreeably with the shipping; and then growing up from all, rises the mellow-tinted brick-built city, roof, and spire, and dome,—a fair and noble sight, indeed, and one not surpassed for a certain quiet and cleanly beauty by any that I know.

Our friends lingered long upon this pretty prospect, and, as inland people of light heart and easy fancy will, the ladies made imagined voyages in each of the more notable vessels they passed,—all cheap and safe trips, occupying half a second apiece. Then they came forward to the bow, that they might not lose any part of the harbor's beauty and variety, and informed themselves of the names of each of the fortressed islands as they passed, and forgot them, being passed, so that to this day Aunt Melissa has the Fort Warren rebel prisoners languishing in Fort Independence. But they made sure of the air of soft repose that hung about each, of that exquisite military neatness which distinguishes them, and which went to Aunt Melissa's housekeeping heart, of the green, thick turf covering the escarpments, of the great guns loafing on the crests of the ramparts and looking out over the water sleepily, of the sentries pacing slowly up and down with their gleaming muskets.

"I never see one of those fellows," says Cousin Frank, "without setting him to the music of that saddest and subtlest of Heine's poems. You know it, Lucy;" and he repeats:—

"Mein Herz, mein Herz is traurig,
Doch lustig leuchtet der Mai;
Ich stehe gelehnt an der Linde,
Hoch auf der alten Bastei.

* * * * *

"Am alten grauen Thurme

Ein Schilderhauschen steht;
Ein rothgerockter Bursche
Dort auf und nieder geht.

"Er spielt mit seiner Flinte,
Sie funkelt im Sonnenroth,
Er prasentirt, und schultert,—
Ich wollt', er schosse mich todt."

"O!" says Cousin Lucy, either because the poignant melancholy of the sentiment has suddenly pierced her, or because she does not quite understand the German,—you never can tell about women. While Frank smiles down upon her in this amiable doubt, their party is approached by the tipsy man who has been making the excursion so merry for the other passengers, in spite of the fact that there is very much to make one sad in him. He is an old man, sweltering in rusty black, a two days' gray beard, and a narrow-brimmed, livid silk hat, set well back upon the nape of his neck. He explains to our friends, as he does to every one whose acquaintance he makes, that he was in former days a seafaring man, and that he has brought his two little grandsons here to show them something about a ship; and the poor old soul helplessly saturates his phrase with the rankest profanity. The boys are somewhat amused by their grandsire's state, being no doubt familiar with it, but a very grim-looking old lady who sits against the pilot-house, and keeps a sharp eye upon all three, and who is also doubtless familiar with the unhappy spectacle, seems not to find it a joke. Her stout matronly umbrella trembles in her hand when her husband draws near, and her eye flashes; but he gives her as wide a berth as he can, returning her glare with a propitiatory drunken smile and a wink to the passengers to let them into the fun. In fact, he is full of humor in his tipsy way, and one after another falls the prey of his free sarcasm, which does not spare the boat or any feature of the excursion. He holds for a long time, by swiftly successive stories of his seafaring days, a very quiet gentleman, who dares neither laugh too loudly nor show indifference for fear of rousing that terrible wit at his expense, and finds his account in looking down at his boots.

"Well, sir," says the deplorable old sinner, "we was forty days out from Liverpool, with a cargo of salt and iron, and we got caught on the Banks in a calm. 'Cap'n,' says I,—I 'us sec'n' mate,—"s they any man aboard this ship knows how to pray?' 'No,' says the cap'n; 'blast yer prayers!' 'Well,' says I, 'cap'n, I'm no hand at all to pray, but I'm goin' to see if prayin' won't git us out 'n this.' And I down on my knees, and I made a first-class prayer; and a breeze sprung up in a minute and carried us smack into Boston."

At this bit of truculent burlesque the quiet man made a bold push, and walked away with a somewhat sickened face, and as no one now intervened between them, the inebriate laid a familiar hand upon Cousin Frank's collar, and said with a wink at his late listener: "Looks like a lerigious man, don't he? I guess I give him a good dose, if he *does* think himself the head-deacon of this boat." And he went on to state his ideas of religion, from which it seemed that he was a person of the most advanced thinking, and believed in nothing worth mentioning.

It is perhaps no worse for an Infidel to be drunk than a Christian, but my friend found this tipsy blasphemer's case so revolting, that he went to the hand-bag, took out the empty claret-bottle, and seeking a solitary corner of the boat, cast the bottle into the water, and felt a thrill of uncommon self-approval as this scapegoat of all the wine at his grocer's bobbed off upon the little waves. "Besides, it saves carrying the bottle home," he thought, not without a half-conscious reserve, that if his penitence were ever too much for him, he could easily abandon it. And without the reflection that the gate is always open behind him, who could consent to enter upon any course of perfect behavior? If good resolutions could not be broken, who would ever have the courage to form them? Would it not be intolerable to be made as good as we ought to be? Then, admirable reader, thank Heaven even for your lapses, since it is so wholesome and saving to be well ashamed of yourself, from time to time.

"What an outrage," said Cousin Frank, in the glow of virtue, as he rejoined the ladies, "that that tipsy rascal should be allowed to go on with his ribaldry. He seems to pervade the whole boat, and to subject everybody to his sway. He's a perfect despot to us helpless sober people,— I wouldn't openly disagree with him on any account. We ought to send a Round Robin to the captain, and ask him to put that religious liberal in irons during the rest of the voyage."

In the mean time, however, the object of his indignation had used up all the conversible material in that part of the boat, and had deviously started for the other end. The elderly woman with the umbrella rose and followed him, somewhat wearily, and with a sadness that appeared more in her movement than in her face; and as the two went down the cabin, did the comical affair look, after all, something like tragedy? My reader, who expects a little novelty in tragedy, and not these stale and common effects, will never think so.

"You'll not pretend, Frank," says Lucy, "that in such an intellectual place as Boston a crowd as large as this can be got together, and no distinguished literary people in it. I know there are some notables aboard: do point them out to me. Pretty near everybody has a literary look."

"Why, that's what we call our Boston look, Cousin Lucy. You needn't have written anything to have it,—it's as general as tubercular consumption, and is the effect of our universal culture and habits of reading. I heard a New-Yorker say once that if you went into a corner grocery in Boston to buy a codfish, the man would ask you how you liked 'Lucille,' whilst he was tying it up. No, no; you mustn't be taken in by that literary look; I'm afraid the real literary men don't always have it. But I *do* see a literary man aboard yonder," he added, craning his neck to one side, and then furtively pointing,—"the most literary man I ever knew, one of the most literary men that ever lived. His whole existence is really bound up in books; he never talks of anything else, and never thinks of anything else, I believe. Look at him,—what kind and pleasant eyes he's got! There, he sees me!" cries Cousin Frank, with a pleasurable excitement. "How d'ye do?" he calls out.

"O Cousin Frank, introduce us," sighs Lucy.

"Not I! He wouldn't thank me. He doesn't care for pretty girls outside of books; he'd be afraid of 'em; he's the bashfullest man alive, and all his heroines are fifty years old, at the least. But before I go any further, tell me solemnly, Lucy, you're not interviewing me? You're not going to write it to a New York newspaper? No? Well, I think it's best to ask, always. Our friend there—he's everybody's friend, if you mean nobody's enemy, by that, not even his own—is really what I say,—the most literary man I ever knew. He loves all epochs and phases of literature, but his passion is the Charles Lamb period and all Lamb's friends. He loves them as if they were living men; and Lamb would have loved him if he could have known him. He speaks rapidly, and rather indistinctly, and when you meet him and say Good day, and you suppose he answers with something about the weather, ten to one he's asking you what you think of Hazlitt's essays on Shakespeare, or Leigh Hunt's Italian Poets, or Lamb's roast pig, or Barry Cornwall's songs. He couldn't get by a bookstall without stopping—for half an hour, at any rate. He knows just when all the new books in town are to be published, and when each bookseller is to get his invoice of old English books. He has no particular address, but if you leave your card for him at any bookstore in Boston, he's sure to get it within two days; and in the summer-time you're apt to meet him on these excursions. Of course, he writes about books, and very tastefully and modestly; there's hardly any of the brand-new immortal English poets, who die off so rapidly, but has had a good word from him; but his heart is with the older fellows, from Chaucer down; and, after the Charles Lamb epoch, I don't know whether he loves better the Elizabethan age or that of Queen Anne. Think of him making me stop the other day at a bookstall, and read through an essay out of the "Spectator!" I did it all for love of him, though money couldn't have persuaded me that I had time; and I'm always telling him lies, and pretending to be as well acquainted as he is with authors I hardly know by name,—he seems so fondly to expect it. He's really almost a disembodied spirit as concerns most mundane interests—his soul is in literature, as a lover's in his mistress's beauty; and in the next world, where, as the Swedenborgians believe, spirits seen at a distance appear like the things they most resemble in disposition, as doves, hawks, goats, lambs, swine, and so on, I'm sure that I shall see his true and kindly soul in the guise of a noble old Folio, quaintly lettered across his back in old English text, *Tom. I.*"

While our friends talked and looked about them, a sudden change had come over the brightness and warmth of the day; the blue heaven had turned a chilly gray, and the water looked harsh and cold. Now, too, they noted that they were drawing near a wooden pier built into the water, and that they had been winding about in a crooked channel between muddy shallows, and that their course was overrun with long, disheveled sea-weed. The shawls had been unstrapped, and the ladies made comfortable in them.

"Ho for the beach!" cried Cousin Frank, with a vehement show of enthusiasm. "Now, then, Aunt Melissa, prepare for the great enjoyment of the day. In a few moments we shall be of the elves

'That on the sand with printless foot
Do chase the ebbing Neptune, and do fly him
When he comes back.'

Come! we shall have three hours on the beach, and that will bring us well into the cool of the evening, and we can return by the last boat."

"As to the cool of the evening," said Aunt Melissa, "I don't know. It's quite cool enough for comfort at present, and I'm sure that anything more wouldn't be wholesome. What's become of our beautiful weather?" she asked, deeply plotting to gain time.

"It's one of our Boston peculiarities, not to say merits," answered Frank, "which you must have noticed already, that we can get rid of a fine day sooner than any other region. While you're saying how lovely it is, a subtle change is wrought, and under skies still blue and a sun still warm the keen spirit of the east wind pierces every nerve, and all the fine weather within you is chilled and extinguished. The gray atmosphere follows, but the day first languishes in yourself. But for this, life in Boston would be insupportably perfect, if this is indeed a drawback. You'd find Bostonians to defend it, I dare say. But this isn't a regular east wind to-day; it's merely our nearness to the sea."

"I think, Franklin," said Aunt Melissa, "that we won't go down to the beach this afternoon," as if she had been there yesterday, and would go to-morrow. "It's too late in the day; and it wouldn't be good for the child, I'm sure."

"Well, aunty, it was you determined us to wait for the boat, and it's your right to say whether we shall leave it or not. I'm very willing not to go ashore. I always find that, after working up to an object with great effort, it's surpassingly sweet to leave it unaccomplished at last. Then it remains forever in the region of the ideal, amongst the songs that never were sung, the pictures that never were painted. Why, in fact, should we force this pleasure? We've eaten our lunch, we've lost the warm heart of the day; why should we poorly drag over to that damp and sullen beach, where we should find three hours very long, when by going back now we can keep intact that glorious image of a day by the sea which we've been cherishing all summer? You're right, Aunt Melissa; we won't go ashore; we will stay here, and respect our illusions."

At heart, perhaps, Lucy did not quite like this retreat; it was not in harmony with the youthful spirit of her sex, but she reflected that she could come again,—O beneficent cheat of Another Time, how much thou sparest us in our over-worked, over-enjoyed world!—she was very comfortable where she was, in a seat commanding a perfect view for the return trip; and she submitted without a murmur. Besides, now that the boat had drawn up to the pier, and discharged part of her passengers, and was waiting to take on others, Lucy was interested in a mass of fluttering dresses and wide-rimmed straw hats that drew down toward the "Rose Standish," and gracefully thronged the pier, and prettily hesitated about, and finally came aboard with laughter and little false cries of terror, attended through all by the New England disproportion of that sex which is so foolish when it is silly. It was a large picnic party which had been spending the day upon the beach, as each of the ladies showed in her face, where, if the roses upon her cheeks were somewhat obscured by the imbrowning seaside sun, a bright pink had been compensatingly bestowed upon the point of her nose. A mysterious quiet fell upon them all when they were got aboard and had taken conspicuous places, which was accounted for presently when a loud shout was heard from the shore, and a man beside an ambulant photographic machine was seen wildly waving his hat. It is impossible to resist a temptation of this kind, and our party all yielded, and posed themselves in striking and characteristic attitudes,—even Aunt Melissa sharing the ambition to appear in a picture which she should never see, and the nurse coming out strong from the abeyance in which she had been held, and lifting the baby high into the air for a good likeness. The frantic gesticulator on the shore gave an impressive wave with both hands, took the cap from the instrument, turned his back, as photographers always do, with that air of hiding their tears, for the brief space that seems so long, and then clapped on the cap again, while a great sigh of relief went up from the whole boat-load of passengers. They were taken.

But the interval had been a luckless one for the "Rose Standish," and when she stirred her wheels, clouds of mud rose to the top of the water, and there was no responsive movement of the boat. She was aground in the falling tide.

"There seems a pretty fair prospect of our spending some time here, after all," said Frank, while the ladies, who had reluctantly given up the idea of staying, were now in a quiver of impatience to be off. The picnic was shifted from side to side; the engine groaned and tugged, Captain

Miles Standish and his crew bestirred themselves vigorously, and at last the boat swung loose, and strode down the sea-weedy channels; while our friends, who had already done the great sights of the harbor, now settled themselves to the enjoyment of its minor traits and beauties. Here and there they passed small parties on the shore, which, with their yachts anchored near, or their boats drawn up from the water, were cooking an out-door meal by a fire that burned bright red upon the sands in the late afternoon air. In such cases, people willingly indulge themselves in saluting whatever craft goes by, and the ladies of these small picnics, as they sat round the fires, kept up a great waving of handkerchiefs, and sometimes cheered the "Rose Standish," though I believe the Bostonians are ordinarily not a demonstrative race. Of course the large picnic on board fluttered multitudinous handkerchiefs in response, both to these people ashore and to those who hailed them from vessels which they met. They did not refuse the politeness even to the passengers on a rival boat when she passed them, though at heart they must have felt some natural pangs at being passed. The water was peopled everywhere by all sorts of sail lagging slowly homeward in the light evening breeze; and on some of the larger vessels there were family groups to be seen, and a graceful smoke, suggestive of supper, curled from the cook's galley. I suppose these ships were chiefly coasting craft, of one kind or another, come from the Provinces at farthest; but to the ignorance and the fancy of our friends, they arrived from all remote and romantic parts of the world,—from India, from China, and from the South Seas, with cargoes of spices and gums and tropical fruits; and I see no reason why one should ever deny himself the easy pleasure they felt in painting the unknown in such lively hues. The truth is, a strange ship, if you will let her, always brings you precious freight, always arrives from Wonderland under the command of Captain Sinbad. How like a beautiful sprite she looks afar off, as if she came from some finer and fairer world than ours! Nay, we will not go out to meet her; we will not go on board; Captain Sinbad shall bring us the invoice of gold-dust, slaves, and rocs' eggs to-night, and we will have some of the eggs for breakfast; or if he never comes, are we not just as rich? But I think these friends of ours got a yet keener pleasure out of the spectacle of a large and stately ship, that with all sails spread moved silently and steadily out toward the open sea. It is yet grander and sweeter to sail toward the unknown than to come from it; and every vessel that leaves port has this destination, and will bear you thither if you will.

"It may be that the gulf shall wash us down;
It may be we shall touch the Happy Isles,
And see the great Achilles, whom we knew,"

absently murmured Lucy, looking on this beautiful apparition.

"But I can't help thinking of Ulysses' cabin-boy, yonder," said Cousin Frank, after a pause; "can you, Aunt Melissa?"

"I don't understand what you're talking about Franklin," answered Aunt Melissa, somewhat severely.

"Why, I mean that there is a poor wretch of a boy on board there, who's run away, and whose heart must be aching just now at the thought of the home he has left. I hope Ulysses will be good to him, and not swear at him for a day or two, or knock him about with a belaying-pin. Just about this time his mother, up in the country, is getting ready his supper, and wondering what's become of him, and torturing herself with hopes that break one by one; and to-night when she goes up to his empty room, having tried to persuade herself that the truant's come back and climbed in at the window"—

"Why, Franklin, this isn't true, is it?" asks Aunt Melissa.

"Well, no, let's pray Heaven it isn't, in this case. It's been true often enough to be false for once."

"What a great, ugly, black object a ship is!" said Cousin Lucy.

Slowly the city rose up against the distance, sharpening all its outlines, and filling in all its familiar details,—like a fact which one dreams is a dream, and which, as the mists of sleep break away, shows itself for reality.

The air grows closer and warmer,—it is the breath of the hot and toil-worn land.

The boat makes her way up through the shipping, seeks her landing, and presently rubs herself affectionately against the wharf. The passengers quickly disperse themselves upon shore, dismissed each with an appropriate sarcasm by the tipsy man, who has had the means of keeping himself drunk throughout, and who now looks to the discharge of the boat's cargo.

As our friends leave the wharf-house behind them, and straggle uneasily, and very conscious of sunburn, up the now silent length of Pearl Street to seek the nearest horse-cars, they are aware of a curious fidgeting of the nurse, who flies from one side of the pavement to the other and violently shifts the baby from one arm to the other.

"What's the matter?" asks Frank; but before the nurse can answer, "Thim little divils," he perceives that the whooping-coughers of the morning have taken the occasion to renew a pleasant acquaintance, and are surrounding the baby and nurse with an atmosphere of whooping-cough.

"I say, friends! we can't stand this, you know," says the anxious father. "We must part some time, and this is a favorable moment. Now I'll give you all this, if you don't come another step!" and he empties out to them, from the hand-bags he carries, the fragments of lunch which the frugal mind of Aunt Melissa had caused her to store there. Upon these the whooping-coughers hurl themselves in a body, and are soon left round the corner. Yet they would have been no disgrace to our party, whose appearance was now most disreputable: Frank and Lucy stalked ahead, with shawls dragging from their arms, the former loaded down with hand-bags and the latter with India-rubbers; Aunt Melissa came next under a burden of bloated umbrellas; the nurse last, with her hat awry, and the baby a caricature of its morning trimness, in her embrace. A day's pleasure is so demoralizing, that no party can stand it, and come out neat and orderly.

"Cousin Frank," asked Lucy, awfully, "what if we should meet the Mayflowers now?"—the Mayflowers being a very ancient and noble Boston family whose acquaintance was the great pride and terror of our friends' lives.

"I should cut them dead," said Frank, and scarcely spoke again till his party dragged slowly up the steps of their minute suburban villa.

At the door his wife met them with a troubled and anxious face.

"Calamities?" asked Frank, desperately.

"O, calamities upon calamities! We've got a lost child in the kitchen," answered Mrs. Sallie.

"O good heavens!" cried her husband. "Adieu, my dreams of repose, so desirable after the quantity of active enjoyment I've had! Well, where is the lost child?"

III—THE EVENING

"Where is the lost child?" repeats Frank, desperately. "Where have you got him?"

"In the kitchen."

"Why in the kitchen?"

"How's baby?" demands Mrs. Sallie, with the incoherent suddenness of her sex, and running halfway down the steps to meet the nurse. "Um, um, um-m-m-m," sounds, which may stand for smothered kisses of rapture and thanksgiving that baby is not a lost child. "Has he been good, Lucy? Take him off and give him some cocoa, Mrs. O'Gonegal," she adds in her business-like way, and with a little push to the combined nurse and baby, while Lucy answers, "O beautiful!" and from that moment, being warned through all her being by something in the other's tone, casts aside the matronly manner which she has worn during the day, and lapses into the comfortable irresponsibility of young-ladyhood.

"What kind of a time did you have?"

"Splendid!" answers Lucy. "Delightful, *I* think," she adds, as if she thought others might not think so.

"I suppose you found Gloucester a quaint old place."

"O," says Frank, "we didn't go to Gloucester; we found that the City Fathers had chartered the boat for the day, so we thought we'd go to Nahant."

"Then you've seen your favorite Gardens of Maolis! What in the world *are* they like?"

"Well; we didn't see the Gardens of Maolis; the Nahant boat was so crowded that we couldn't think of going on her, and so we decided we'd drive over to the Liverpool Wharf and go down to Nantasket Beach."

"That was nice. I'm so glad on Aunt Melissa's account. It's much better to see the ocean from a long beach than from those Nahant rocks."

"That's what *I* said. But, you know, when we got to the wharf the boat had just left."

"You *don't* mean it! Well, then, what under the canopy *did* you do?"

"Why, we sat down in the wharf-house, and waited from nine o'clock till half-past two for the next boat."

"Well, I'm glad you didn't back out, at any rate. You did show pluck, you poor things! I hope you enjoyed the beach after you *did* get there."

"Why," says Frank, looking down, "we never got there."

"Never got there!" gasps Mrs. Sallie. "Didn't you go down on the afternoon boat?"

"Yes."

"Why didn't you get to the beach, then?"

"We didn't go ashore."

"Well, that's *like* you, Frank."

"It's a great deal more like Aunt Melissa," answers Frank. "The air felt so raw and chilly by the time we reached the pier, that she declared the baby would perish if it was taken to the beach. Besides, nothing would persuade her that Nantasket Beach was at all different from Liverpool Wharf."

"Never mind, never mind!" says Mrs. Sallie. "I don't wish to hear anything more. That's your idea of a day's pleasure, is it? I call it a day's disgrace, a day's miserable giving-up. There, go in, go in; I'm ashamed of you all. Don't let the neighbors see you, for pity's sake.—We keep him in the kitchen," she continues, recurring to Frank's long-unanswered question concerning the lost child, "because he prefers it as being the room nearest to the closet where the cookies are. He's taken advantage of our sympathies to refuse everything but cookies."

"I suppose that's one of the rights of lost childhood," comments Frank, languidly; "there's no law that can compel him to touch even cracker."

"Well, you'd better go down and see what *you* can make of him. He's driven *us* all wild."

So Frank descends to the region now redolent of the preparing tea, and finds upon a chair, in the middle of the kitchen floor, a very forlorn little figure of a boy, mutely munching a sweet-cake, while now and then a tear steals down his cheeks and moistens the grimy traces of former tears. He and baby are, in the mean time regarding each other with a steadfast glare, the cook and the nurse supporting baby in this rite of hospitality.

"Well, my little man," says his host, "how did you get here?"

The little man, perhaps because he is heartily sick of the question, is somewhat slow to answer that there was a fire; and that he ran after the steamer; and a girl found him and brought him up here.

"And that's all the blessed thing you can get out of him," says cook; and the lost boy looks as if he felt cook to be perfectly right.

In spite of the well-meant endeavors of the household to wash him and brush him, he is still a dreadfully travel-stained little boy, and he is powdered in every secret crease and wrinkle by that dust of old Charlesbridge, of which we always speak with an air of affected disgust, and a feeling of ill-concealed pride in an abomination so strikingly and peculiarly our own. He looks very much as if he had been following fire-engines about the streets of our learned and pulverous suburb ever since he could walk, and he certainly seems to feel himself in trouble to a certain degree; but there is easily imaginable in his bearing a conviction that after all the chief care is with others, and that, though unhappy, he is not responsible. The principal victim of his sorrows is also penetrated by this opinion, and after gazing forlornly upon him for a while, asks mechanically, "What's your name?"

"Freddy," is the laconic answer.

"Freddy—?" trying with an artful inflection to lead him on to his surname.

"Freddy," decidedly and conclusively.

"O, bless me! What's the name of the street your papa lives on?"

This problem is far too deep for Freddy, and he takes a bite of sweet-cake in sign that he does not think of solving it. Frank looks at him gloomily for a moment, and then determines that he can grapple with the difficulty more successfully after he has had tea. "Send up the supper, Bridget. I think, my dear," he says, after they have sat down, "we'd better all question our lost child when we've finished."

So, when they have finished, they have him up in the sitting-room, and the inquisition begins.

"Now, Freddy," his host says, with a cheerful air of lifelong friendship and confidence, "you know that everybody has got two names. Of course your first name is Freddy, and it's a very pretty name. Well, I want you to think real hard, and then tell me what your other name is, so I can take you back to your mamma."

At this allusion the child looks round on the circle of eager and compassionate faces, and begins to shed tears and to wring all hearts.

"What's your name?" asks Frank, cheerfully,—"your *other* name, you know?"

"Freddy," sobbed the forlorn creature.

"O good heaven! this'll never do," groaned the chief inquisitor. "Now, Freddy, try not to cry. What is your papa's name,—Mr.—?" with the leading inflection as before.

"Papa," says Freddy.

"O, that'll never do! Not Mr. Papa?"

"Yes," persists Freddy.

"But, Freddy," interposes Mrs. Sallie, as her husband falls

back baffled, "when ladies come to see your mamma, what do they call her? Mrs.—?" adopting Frank's alluring inflection.

"Mrs. Mamma," answers Freddy, confirmed in his error by this course; and a secret dismay possesses his questioners. They skirmish about him with every sort of query; they try to entrap him into some kind of revelation by apparently irrelevant remarks; they plan ambuscades and surprises; but Freddy looks vigilantly round upon them, and guards his personal history from every approach, and seems in every way so to have the best of it, that it is almost exasperating.

"Kindness has proved futile," observes Frank, "and I think we ought as a last resort, before yielding ourselves to despair, to use intimidation. Now, Fred," he says, with sudden and terrible severity, "what's your father's name?"

The hapless little soul is really moved to an effort of memory by this, and blubbers out something that proves in the end to resemble the family name, though for the present it is merely a puzzle of unintelligible sounds."

"Blackman?" cries Aunt Melissa, catching desperately at these sounds.

On this, all the man and brother is roused in Freddy's bosom, and he roars fiercely, "No! he ain't a black man! He's white!"

"I give it up," says Frank, who has been looking for his hat. "I'm afraid we can't make anything out of him; and I'll have to go and report the case to the police. But, put him to bed, do, Sallie; he's dropping with sleep."

So he went out, of course supported morally by a sense of

duty, but I am afraid also by a sense of adventure in some degree. It is not every day that, in so quiet a place as Charlesbridge, you can have a lost child cast upon your sympathies; and I believe that when an appeal is not really agonizing, we like so well to have our sympathies touched, we favorites of the prosperous commonplace, that most of us would enter eagerly into a pathetic case of this kind, even after a day's pleasure. Such was certainly the mood of my friend, and he unconsciously prepared himself for an equal interest on the part of the police; but this was an error. The police heard his statement with all proper attention, and wrote it in full upon the station-slate, but they showed no feeling whatever, and behaved as if they valued a lost child no more than a child snug at home in his own crib. They said that no doubt his parents would be asking at the police-stations for him during the night, and, as if my friend would otherwise have thought of putting him into the street, they suggested that he should just keep the lost child till he was sent for. Modestly enough Frank proposed that they should make some inquiry for his parents, and was answered by the question whether they could take a man off his beat for that purpose; and remembering that beats in Charlesbridge were of such vastness that during his whole residence there he had never yet seen a policeman on his street, he was obliged to own to himself that his proposal was absurd. He felt the need of reinstating himself by something more sensible, and so he said he thought he would go down to the Port and leave word at the station there; and the police tacitly assenting to this he went.

I who have sometimes hinted that the Square is not a centre of gayety, or a scene of the greatest activity by day, feel it right to say that it has some modest charms of its own on a summer's night, about the hour when Frank passed through it, when the post-office has just been shut, and when the different groups that haunt the place in front of the closing shops have dwindled to the loungers fit though few who will keep it well into the night, and may there be found, by the passenger on the last horse-car out from Boston, wrapt in a kind of social silence, and honorably attended by the policeman whose favored beat is in that neighborhood. They seem a feature of the bygone village life of Charlesbridge, and accord pleasantly with the town-pump and the public horse-trough, and the noble elm that by night droops its boughs so pensively, and probably dreams of its happy younger days when there were no canker-worms in the world. Sometimes this choice company sits on the curbing that goes round the terrace at the elm-tree's foot, and then I envy every soul in it,—so tranquil it seems, so cool, so careless, so morrowless. I cannot see the faces of that luxurious society, but there I imagine is the local albino, and a certain blind man, who resorts thither much by day, and makes a strange kind of jest of his own, with a flicker of humor upon his sightless face, and a faith that others less unkindly treated by nature will be able to see the point apparently not always discernible to himself. Late at night I have a fancy that the darkness puts him on an equality with other wits, and that he enjoys his own brilliancy as well as any one.

At the Port station Frank was pleased and soothed by the tranquil air of the policeman, who sat in his shirt-sleeves outside the door, and seemed to announce, by his attitude of final disoccupation, that crimes and misdemeanors were no more. This officer at once showed a desirable interest in the case. He put on his blue coat that he might listen to the whole story in a proper figure, and then he took down the main points on the slate, and said that they would send word round to the other stations in the city, and the boy's parents could hardly help hearing of him that night.

Returned home, Frank gave his news, and then he and Mrs. Sallie went up to look at the lost child as he slept. The sumptuous diet to which he had confined himself from the first seemed to agree with him perfectly, for he slept unbrokenly, and apparently without a consciousness of his woes. On a chair lay his clothes, in a dusty little pathetic heap; they were well-kept clothes, except for the wrong his wanderings had done them, and they showed a motherly care here and there, which it was not easy to look at with composure. The spectators of his sleep both thought of the curious chance that had thrown this little one into their charge, and considered that he was almost as completely a gift of the Unknown as if he had been following a steamer in another planet, and had thence dropped into their yard. His helplessness in accounting for himself was as affecting as that of the sublimest metaphysician; and no learned man, no superior intellect, no subtle inquirer among us lost children of the divine, forgotten home, could have been less able to say how or whence he came to be just where he found himself. We wander away and away; the dust of the road-side gathers upon us; and when some strange shelter receives us, we lie down to our sleep, inarticulate, and haunted with dreams of memory, or the memory of dreams, knowing scarcely more of the past than of the future.

"What a strange world!" sighed Mrs. Sallie; and then, as this was a mood far too speculative for her, she recalled herself to practical life suddenly. "If we should have to adopt this child, Frank"—

"Why, bless my soul, we're not obliged to adopt him! Even a lost child can't demand that."

"We shall adopt him, if they don't come for him. And now, I want to know" (Mrs. Sallie spoke as if the adoption had been effected) "whether we shall give him our name, or some other?"

"Well, I don't know. It's the first child I've ever adopted," said Frank "and upon my word, I can't say whether you have to give him a new name or not. In fact, if I'd thought of this affair of a name, I'd never have adopted him. It's the greatest part of the burden, and if his father will only come for him, I'll give him up without a murmur."

In the interval that followed the proposal of this alarming difficulty, and while he sat and waited vaguely for whatever should be going to happen next, Frank was not able to repress a sense of personal resentment towards the little vagrant sleeping so carelessly there, though at the bottom of his heart there was all imaginable tenderness for him. In the fantastic character which, to his weariness, the day's pleasure took on, it seemed an extraordinary unkindness of fate that this lost child should have been kept in reserve for him after all the rest; and he had so small consciousness of bestowing shelter and charity, and so profound a feeling of having himself been turned out of house and home by some surprising and potent agency, that if the lost child had been a regiment of Fenians billeted upon him, it could not have oppressed him more. While he remained perplexed in this perverse sentiment of invasion and dispossession, "Hark!" said Mrs. Sallie, "what's that?"

It was a noise of dragging and shuffling on the walk in front of the house, and a low, hoarse whispering.

"I don't know," said Frank, "but from the kind of pleasure I've got out of it so far, I should say that this holiday was capable of an earthquake before midnight."

"Listen!"

They listened, as they must, and heard the outer darkness rehearse a raucous dialogue between an unseen Bill and Jim, who were the more terrible to the imagination from being so realistically named, and who seemed to have in charge some nameless third person, a mute actor in the invisible scene. There was doubt, which he uttered, in the mind of Jim, whether they could get this silent comrade along much farther without carrying him; and there was a growling assent from Bill that he *was* pretty far gone, that was a fact, and that maybe Jim *had* better go for the wagon; then there were quick, retreating steps; and then there was a profound silence, in which the audience of this strange drama sat thrilled and speechless. The effect was not less dreadful when there rose a dull sound, as of a helpless body rubbing against the fence, and at last lowered heavily to the ground.

"O!" cried Mrs. Sallie. "Do go out and help. He's dying!"

But even as she spoke the noise of wheels was heard. A wagon stopped before the door; there came a tugging and lifting, with a sound as of crunching gravel, and then a "There!" of great relief.

"Frank!" said Mrs. Sallie very solemnly, "if you don't go out and help those men, I'll never forgive you."

Really, the drama had grown very impressive; it was a mystery, to say the least; and so it must remain forever, for when Frank, infected at last by Mrs. Sallie's faith in tragedy, opened the door and offered his tardy services, the wagon was driven rapidly away without reply. They never learned what it had all been; and I think that if one actually honors mysteries, it is best not to look into them. How much finer, after all, if you have such a thing as this happen before your door at midnight, not to throw any light upon it! Then your probable tipsy man cannot be proved other than a tragical presence, which you can match with any inscrutable creation of fiction; and if you should ever come to write a romance, as one is very liable to do in this age, there is your unknown, a figure of strange and fearful interest, made to your hand, and capable of being used, in or out of the body, with a very gloomy effect.

While our friends yet trembled with this sensation, quick steps ascended to their door, and then followed a sharp, anxious tug at the bell.

"Ah!" cried Frank, prophetically, "here's the father of our adopted son;" and he opened the door.

The gentleman who appeared there could scarcely frame the question to which Frank replied so cheerfully: "O yes; he's here, and snug in bed, and fast asleep. Come up-stairs and look at him. Better let him be till morning, and then come after him," he added, as they looked down a moment on the little sleeper.

"O no, I couldn't," said the father, *con expressione*; and then he told how he had heard of this child's whereabouts at the Port station, and had hurried to get him, and how his mother did not know he was found yet, and was almost wild about him. They had no idea how he had got lost, and his own blind story was the only tale of his adventure that ever became known.

By this time his father had got the child partly awake, and the two men were dressing him in men's clumsy fashion; and finally they gave it up, and rolled him in a shawl. The father lifted the slight burden, and two small arms fell about his neck. The weary child slept again.

"How has he behaved?" asked the father.

"Like a little hero," said Frank, "but he's been a cormorant for cookies. I think it right to tell you, in case he shouldn't be very brilliant to-morrow, that he wouldn't eat a bit of anything else."

The father said he was the life of their house; and Frank said he knew how that was,—that he had a life of the house of his own; and then the father thanked him very simply and touchingly, and with the decent New England self-restraint, which is doubtless so much better than any sort of effusion. "Say good-night to the gentleman, Freddy," he said at the door; and Freddy with closed eyes murmured a good-night from far within the land of dreams, and then was borne away to the house out of which the life had wandered with his little feet.

"I don't know, Sallie," said Frank, when he had given all the eagerly demanded particulars about the child's father,—"I don't know whether I should want many such holidays as this, in the course of the summer. On the whole, I think I'd better overwork myself and not take any relaxation, if I mean to live long. And yet I'm not sure that the day's been altogether a failure, though all our purposes of enjoyment have miscarried. I didn't plan to find a lost child here, when I got home, and I'm afraid I haven't had always the most Christian feeling towards him; but he's really the saving grace of the affair; and if this were a little comedy I had been playing, I should turn him to account with the jaded audience, and advancing to the foot-lights, should say, with my hand on my waistcoat, and a neat bow, that although every hope of the day had been disappointed, and nothing I had meant to do had been done, yet the man who had ended at midnight by restoring a lost child to the arms of its father, must own that, in spite of adverse fortune, he had enjoyed A Day's Pleasure."

W. D. Howells

A ROMANCE OF REAL LIFE

It was long past the twilight hour, which has been already
mentioned as so oppressive in suburban places, and it was
even too late for visitors, when a resident, whom I shall
briefly describe as a Contributor to the magazines, was
startled by a ring at his door. As any thoughtful person
would have done upon the like occasion, he ran over his
acquaintance in his mind, speculating whether it were
such or such a one, and dismissing the whole list of
improbabilities, before he laid down the book he was
reading, and answered the bell. When at last he did this,
he was rewarded by the apparition of an utter stranger on
his threshold,—a gaunt figure of forlorn and curious
smartness towering far above him, that jerked him a nod
of the head, and asked if Mr. Hapford lived there. The
face which the lamp-light revealed was remarkable for a
harsh two days' growth of beard, and a single bloodshot
eye; yet it was not otherwise a sinister countenance, and
there was something in the strange presence that appealed
and touched. The contributor, revolving the facts vaguely
in his mind, was not sure, after all, that it was not the
man's clothes rather than his expression that softened him
toward the rugged visage: they were so tragically cheap,
and the misery of helpless needlewomen, and the poverty
and ignorance of the purchaser, were so apparent in their
shabby newness, of which they appeared still conscious
enough to have led the way to the very window, in the

Semitic quarter of the city, where they had lain ticketed, "This nobby suit for $15."

But the stranger's manner put both his face and his clothes out of mind, and claimed a deeper interest when, being answered that the person for whom he asked did not live there, he set his bristling lips hard together, and sighed heavily.

"They told me," he said, in a hopeless way, "that he lived on this street, and I've been to every other house. I'm very anxious to find him, Cap'n,"—the contributor, of course, had no claim to the title with which he was thus decorated,—"for I've a daughter living with him, and I want to see her; I've just got home from a two years' voyage, and"—there was a struggle of the Adam's-apple in the man's gaunt throat—"I find she's about all there is left of my family."

How complex is every human motive! This contributor had been lately thinking, whenever he turned the pages of some foolish traveller,—some empty prattler of Southern or Eastern lands, where all sensation was long ago exhausted, and the oxygen has perished from every sentiment, so has it been breathed and breathed again,—that nowadays the wise adventurer sat down beside his own register and waited for incidents to seek him out. It seemed to him that the cultivation of a patient and receptive spirit was the sole condition needed to insure the occurrence of all manner of surprising facts within the range of one's own personal knowledge; that not only the Greeks were at our doors, but the fairies and the genii, and all the people of romance, who had but to be hospitably treated in order to develop the deepest interest of fiction, and to become the characters of plots so ingenious that the most cunning invention were poor beside them. I myself am not so confident of this, and

W. D. Howells

would rather trust Mr. Charles Reade, say, for my amusement than any chance combination of events. But I should be afraid to say how much his pride in the character of the stranger's sorrows, as proof of the correctness of his theory, prevailed with the contributor to ask him to come in and sit down; though I hope that some abstract impulse of humanity, some compassionate and unselfish care for the man's misfortunes as misfortunes, was not wholly wanting. Indeed, the helpless simplicity with which he had confided his case might have touched a harder heart. "Thank you," said the poor fellow, after a moment's hesitation. "I believe I will come in. I've been on foot all day, and after such a long voyage it makes a man dreadfully sore to walk about so much. Perhaps you can think of a Mr. Hapford living somewhere in the neighborhood."

He sat down, and, after a pondering silence, in which he had remained with his head fallen upon his breast, "My name is Jonathan Tinker," he said, with the unaffected air which had already impressed the contributor, and as if he felt that some form of introduction was necessary, "and the girl that I want to find is Julia Tinker." Then he added, resuming the eventful personal history which the listener exulted, while he regretted, to hear: "You see, I shipped first to Liverpool, and there I heard from my family; and then I shipped again for Hong-Kong, and after that I never heard a word: I seemed to miss the letters everywhere. This morning, at four o'clock, I left my ship as soon as she had hauled into the dock, and hurried up home. The house was shut, and not a soul in it; and I didn't know what to do, and I sat down on the doorstep to wait till the neighbors woke up, to ask them what had become of my family. And the first one come out he told me my wife had been dead a year and a half, and the baby I'd never seen, with her; and one of my boys was dead; and he didn't know where the rest of the children was, but he'd heard two of the little ones was with a family in the city."

The man mentioned these things with the half-apologetic air observable in a certain kind of Americans when some accident obliges them to confess the infirmity of the natural feelings. They do not ask your sympathy, and you offer it quite at your own risk, with a chance of having it thrown back upon your hands. The contributor assumed the risk so far as to say, "Pretty rough!" when the stranger caused; and perhaps these homely words were best suited to reach the homely heart. The man's quavering lips closed hard again, a kind of spasm passed over his dark face, and then two very small drops of brine shone upon his weather-worn cheeks. This demonstration, into which he had been surprised, seemed to stand for the passion of tears into which the emotional races fall at such times. He opened his lips with a kind of dry click, and went on:—

"I hunted about the whole forenoon in the city, and at last I found the children. I'd been gone so long they didn't know me, and somehow I thought the people they were with weren't over-glad I'd turned up. Finally the oldest child told me that Julia was living with a Mr. Hapford on this street, and I started out here to-night to look her up. If I can find her, I'm all right. I can get the family together, then, and start new."

"It seems rather odd," mused the listener aloud, "that the neighbors let them break up so, and that they should all scatter as they did."

"Well, it ain't so curious as it seems, Cap'n. There was money for them at the owners', all the time; I'd left part of my wages when I sailed; but they didn't know how to get at it, and what could a parcel of children do? Julia's a good girl, and when I find her I'm all right."

The writer could only repeat that there was no Mr. Hapford living on that street, and never had been, so far as he knew. Yet there might be such a person in the neighborhood; and they would go out together, and ask at some of the houses about. But the stranger must first take a glass of wine; for he looked used up.

The sailor awkwardly but civilly enough protested that he did not want to give so much trouble, but took the glass, and, as he put it to his lips, said formally, as if it were a toast or a kind of grace, "I hope I may have the opportunity of returning the compliment." The contributor thanked him; though, as he thought of all the circumstances of the case, and considered the cost at which the stranger had come to enjoy his politeness, he felt little eagerness to secure the return of the compliment at the same price, and added, with the consequence of another set phrase, "Not at all." But the thought had made him the more anxious to befriend the luckless soul fortune had cast in his way; and so the two sallied out together, and rang door-bells wherever lights were still seen burning in the windows, and asked the astonished people who answered their summons whether any Mr. Hapford were known to live in the neighborhood.

And although the search for this gentleman proved vain, the contributor could not feel that an expedition which set familiar objects in such novel light? was altogether a failure. He entered so intimately into the cares and anxieties of his *protege,* that at times he felt himself in some inexplicable sort a shipmate of Jonathan Tinker, and almost personally a partner of his calamities. The estrangement of all things which takes place, within doors and without, about midnight may have helped to cast this doubt upon his identity;—he seemed to be visiting now for the first time the streets and neighborhoods nearest his own, and his feet stumbled over the accustomed walks. In his quality of houseless wanderer, and—so far as appeared to others—possibly worthless vagabond, he also got a new and instructive effect upon the faces which, in his real character, he knew so well by their looks of neighborly greeting; and it is his belief that the first hospitable prompting of the human heart is to shut the door in the eyes of homeless strangers who present themselves after eleven o'clock. By that time the servants are all abed, and the gentleman of the house answers the bell, and looks out with a loath and bewildered face, which gradually changes to one of suspicion, and of wonder as to what those fellows can possibly want of *him,* till at last the prevailing expression is one of contrite desire to atone for the first reluctance by any sort of service. The contributor professes to have observed these changing phases in the visages of those whom he that night called from their dreams, or arrested in the act of going to bed; and he drew the conclusion—very proper for his imaginable connection with the garroting and other adventurous brotherhoods—that the most flattering moment for knocking on the head people who answer a late ring at night is either in their first selfish bewilderment, or their final self-abandonment to their better impulses. It does not seem to have occurred to him that he would himself have been a much more favorable subject for the predatory arts that any of his neighbors, if his shipmate, the unknown companion of his researches for Mr. Hapford, had been at all so minded. But the faith of the gaunt giant upon which he reposed was good, and the contributor continued to wander about with him in perfect safety. Not a soul among those they asked had ever heard of a Mr. Hapford,—far less of a Julia Tinker living with him. But they all listened to the contributor's explanation with interest and eventual sympathy; and in truth,— briefly told, with a word now and then thrown in by Jonathan Tinker, who kept at the bottom of the steps, showing like a gloomy spectre in the night, or, in his grotesque length and gauntness, like the other's shadow cast there by the lamplight,—it was a story which could hardly fail to awaken pity.

At last, after ringing several bells where there were no lights, in the mere wantonness of good-will, and going away before they could be answered (it would be entertaining to know what dreams they caused the sleepers within), there seemed to be nothing for it but to give up the search till morning, and go to the main street and wait for the last horse-car to the city.

There, seated upon the curbstone, Jonathan Tinker, being plied with a few leading questions, told in hints and scraps the story of his hard life, which was at present that of a second mate, and had been that of a cabin-boy and of a seaman before the mast. The second mate's place he held to be the hardest aboard ship. You got only a few dollars more than the men, and you did not rank with the officers; you took your meals alone, and in every thing you belonged by yourself. The men did not respect you, and sometimes the captain abused you awfully before the passengers. The hardest captain that Jonathan Tinker ever sailed with was Captain Gooding of the Cape. It had got to be so that no man would ship second mate under Captain Gooding; and Jonathan Tinker was with him only one voyage. When he had been home awhile, he saw an advertisement for a second mate, and he went round to the owners'. They had kept it secret who the captain was; but there was Captain Gooding in the owners' office. "Why, here's the man, now, that I want for a second mate," said he, when Jonathan Tinker entered; "he knows me."—"Captain Gooding, I know you 'most too well to want to sail under you," answered Jonathan. "I might go if I hadn't been with you one voyage too many already."

"And then the men!" said Jonathan, "the men coming

aboard drunk, and having to be pounded sober! And the hardest of the fight falls on the second mate! Why, there isn't an inch of me that hasn't been cut over or smashed into a jell. I've had three ribs broken; I've got a scar from a knife on my cheek; and I've been stabbed bad enough, half a dozen times, to lay me up."

Here he gave a sort of desperate laugh, as if the notion of so much misery and such various mutilation were too grotesque not to be amusing. "Well, what can you do?" he went on. "If you don't strike, the men think you're afraid of them; and so you have to begin hard and go on hard. I always tell a man, 'Now, my man, I always begin with a man the way I mean to keep on. You do your duty and you're all right. But if you don't'—Well, the men ain't Americans any more,—Dutch, Spaniards, Chinese, Portuguee,—and it ain't like abusing a white man."

Jonathan Tinker was plainly part of the horrible tyranny which we all know exists on shipboard; and his listener respected him the more that, though he had heart enough to be ashamed of it, he was too honest not to own it.

Why did he still follow the sea? Because he did not know what else to do. When he was younger, he used to love it, but now he hated it. Yet there was not a prettier life in the world if you got to be captain. He used to hope for that once, but not now; though he *thought* he could navigate a ship. Only let him get his family together again, and he would—yes, he would—try to do something ashore.

No car had yet come in sight, and so the contributor suggested that they should walk to the car-office, and look in the "Directory," which is kept there, for the name of Hapford, in search of whom it had already been arranged that they should renew their acquaintance on the morrow. Jonathan Tinker, when they had reached the office, heard

W. D. Howells

with constitutional phlegm that the name of the Hapford, for whom he inquired was not in the "Directory." "Never mind," said the other; "come round to my house in the morning. We'll find him yet." So they parted with a shake of the hand, the second mate saying that he believed he should go down to the vessel and sleep aboard,—if he could sleep,—and murmuring at the last moment the hope of returning the compliment, while the other walked homeward, weary as to the flesh, but, in spite of his sympathy for Jonathan Tinker, very elate in spirit. The truth is,—and however disgraceful to human nature, let the truth still be told,—he had recurred to his primal satisfaction in the man as calamity capable of being used for such and such literary ends, and, while he pitied him, rejoiced in him as an episode of real life quite as striking and complete as anything in fiction. It was literature made to his hand. Nothing could be better, he mused; and once more he passed the details of the story in review, and beheld all those pictures which the poor fellow's artless words had so vividly conjured up: he saw him leaping ashore in the gray summer dawn as soon as the ship hauled into the dock, and making his way, with his vague sea-legs unaccustomed to the pavements, up through the silent and empty city streets; he imagined the tumult of fear and hope which the sight of the man's home must have caused in him, and the benumbing shock of finding it blind and deaf to all his appeals; he saw him sitting down upon what had been his own threshold, and waiting in a sort of bewildered patience till the neighbors should be awake, while the noises of the streets gradually arose, and the wheels began to rattle over the stones, and the milk-man and the ice-man came and went, and the waiting figure began to be stared at, and to challenge the curiosity of the passing policeman; he fancied the opening of the neighbor's door, and the slow, cold understanding of the case; the manner, whatever it was, in which the sailor was told that one year before his wife had died, with her babe, and that his children were scattered, none knew where. As the contributor dwelt pityingly upon these things, but at the same time estimated their aesthetic value one by one, he drew near the head of his street, and found himself a few paces behind a boy slouching onward through the night, to whom he called out, adventurously, and with no real hope of information,—

"Do you happen to know anybody on this street by the name of Hapford?"

"Why no, not in this town," said the boy; but he added that there was a street of the same name in a neighboring suburb, and that there was a Hapford living on it.

"By Jove!" thought the contributor, "this is more like literature than ever;" and he hardly knew whether to be more provoked at his own stupidity in not thinking of a street of the same name in the next village, or delighted at the element of fatality which the fact introduced into the story; for Tinker, according to his own account, must have landed from the cars a few rods from the very door he was seeking, and so walked farther and farther from it every moment. He thought the case so curious, that he laid it briefly before the boy, who, however he might have been inwardly affected, was sufficiently true to the national traditions not to make the smallest conceivable outward sign of concern in it.

At home, however, the contributor related his adventures and the story of Tinker's life, adding the fact that he had just found out where Mr. Hapford lived. "It was the only touch wanting," said he; "the whole thing is now perfect."

"It's *too* perfect," was answered from a sad enthusiasm. "Don't speak of it! I can't take it in."

W. D. Howells

"But the question is," said the contributor, penitently taking himself to task for forgetting the hero of these excellent misfortunes in his delight at their perfection, "how am I to sleep to-night, thinking of that poor soul's suspense and uncertainty? Never mind,—I'll be up early, and run over and make sure that it is Tinker's Hapford, before he gets out here, and have a pleasant surprise for him. Would it not be a justifiable *coup de theatre* to fetch his daughter here, and let her answer his ring at the door when he comes in the morning?"

This plan was discouraged. "No, no; let them meet in their own way. Just take him to Hapford's house and leave him."

"Very well. But he's too good a character to lose sight of. He's got to come back here and tell us what he intends to do."

The birds, next morning, not having had the second mate on their minds either as an unhappy man or a most fortunate episode, but having slept long and soundly, were singing in a very sprightly way in the way-side trees; and the sweetness of their notes made the contributor's heart light as he climbed the hill and rang at Mr. Hapford's door.

The door was opened by a young girl of fifteen or sixteen, whom he knew at a glance for the second mate's daughter, but of whom, for form's sake, he asked if there were a girl named Julia Tinker living there.

"My name's Julia Tinker," answered the maid, who had rather a disappointing face.

"Well," said the contributor, "your father's got back from his Hong-Kong voyage."

"Hong-Kong voyage?" echoed the girl, with a stare of helpless inquiry, but no other visible emotion.

"Yes. He had never heard of your mother's death. He came home yesterday morning, and was looking for you all day."

Julia Tinker remained open-mouthed but mute; and the other was puzzled at the want of feeling shown, which he could not account for even as a national trait. "Perhaps there's some mistake," he said.

"There must be," answered Julia: "my father hasn't been to sea for a good many years. *My* father," she added, with a diffidence indescribably mingled with a sense of distinction,—"*my* father's in State's Prison. What kind of looking man was this?"

The contributor mechanically described him.

Julia Tinker broke into a loud, hoarse laugh. "Yes, it's him, sure enough." And then, as if the joke were too good to keep: "Miss Hapford, Miss Hapford, father's got out. Do come here!" she called into a back room.

When Mrs. Hapford appeared, Julia fell back, and, having deftly caught a fly on the door-post, occupied herself in plucking it to pieces, while she listened to the conversation of the others.

"It's all true enough," said Mrs. Hapford, when the writer had recounted the moving story of Jonathan Tinker, "so far as the death of his wife and baby goes. But he hasn't been to sea for a good many years, and he must have just come out of State's Prison, where he was put for bigamy. There's always two sides to a story, you know; but they say it broke his first wife's heart, and she died. His friends don't want him to find his children, and this girl especially."

"He's found his children in the city," said the contributor, gloomily, being at a loss what to do or say, in view of the wreck of his romance.

"O, he's found 'em has he?" cried Julia, with heightened amusement. "Then he'll have me next, if I don't pack and go."

"I'm very, very sorry," said the contributor, secretly resolved never to do another good deed, no matter how temptingly the opportunity presented itself. "But you may depend he won't find out from *me* where you are. Of course I had no earthly reason for supposing his story was not true."

"Of course," said kind-hearted Mrs. Hapford, mingling a drop of honey with the gall in the contributor's soul, "you only did your duty."

And indeed, as he turned away he did not feel altogether without compensation. However Jonathan Tinker had fallen in his esteem as a man, he had even risen as literature. The episode which had appeared so perfect in its pathetic phases did not seem less finished as a farce; and this person, to whom all things of every-day life presented themselves in periods more or less rounded, and capable of use as facts or illustrations, could not but rejoice in these new incidents, as dramatically fashioned as the rest. It occurred to him that, wrought into a story, even better use might be made of the facts now than before, for they had developed questions of character and of human nature which could not fail to interest. The more he pondered upon his acquaintance with Jonathan Tinker, the more fascinating the erring mariner became, in his complex truth and falsehood, his delicately blending shades of artifice and *naivete*. He must, it was felt, have believed to a certain point in his own inventions: nay, starting with that groundwork of truth,—the fact that his wife was really dead, and that he had not seen his family for two years,—why should he not place implicit faith in all the fictions reared upon it? It was probable that he felt a real sorrow for her loss, and that he found a fantastic consolation in depicting the circumstances of her death so that they should look like his inevitable misfortunes rather than his faults. He might well have repented his offense during those two years of prison; and why should he not now cast their dreariness and shame out of his memory, and replace them with the freedom and adventure of a two years' voyage to China,—so probable, in all respects, that the fact should appear an impossible nightmare? In the experiences of his life he had abundant material to furnish forth the facts of such a voyage, and in the weariness and lassitude that should follow a day's walking equally after a two years' voyage and two years' imprisonment, he had as much physical proof in favor of one hypothesis as the other. It was doubtless true, also, as he said, that he had gone to his house at dawn, and sat down on the threshold of his ruined home; and perhaps he felt the desire he had expressed to see his daughter, with a purpose of beginning life anew; and it may have cost him a veritable pang when he found that his little ones did not know him. All the sentiments of the situation were such as might persuade a lively fancy of the truth of its own inventions; and as he heard these continually repeated by the contributor in their search for Mr. Hapford, they must have acquired an objective force and repute scarcely to be resisted. At the same time, there were touches of nature throughout Jonathan Tinker's narrative which could not fail to take the faith of another. The contributor, in reviewing it, thought it particularly charming that his mariner had not overdrawn himself, or attempted to paint his character otherwise than as it probably was; that he had shown his ideas and practices of life to be those of a second mate, nor more nor less, without the gloss of regret or the pretenses to refinement that might be pleasing to the supposed philanthropist with whom he had fallen in. Captain Gooding was of course a true portrait; and there was nothing in Jonathan Tinker's statement of the relations of a second mate to his superiors and his inferiors which did not agree perfectly with what the contributor had just read in "Two Years before the Mast,"—a book which had possibly cast its glamour upon the adventure. He admired also the just and perfectly characteristic air of grief in the bereaved husband and father,—those occasional escapes from the sense of loss into a brief hilarity and forgetfulness, and those relapses into the hovering gloom, which every one has observed in this poor, crazy human nature when oppressed by sorrow, and which it would have been hard to simulate. But, above all, he exulted in that supreme stroke of the imagination given by the second mate when, at parting, he said he believed he would go down and sleep on board the vessel. In view of this, the State's Prison theory almost appeared a malign and foolish scandal.

Yet even if this theory were correct, was the second mate wholly answerable for beginning his life again with the imposture he had practiced? The contributor had either so fallen in love with the literary advantages of his forlorn deceiver that he would see no moral obliquity in him, or he had touched a subtler verity at last in pondering the affair. It seemed now no longer a farce, but had a pathos which, though very different from that of its first aspect, was hardly less tragical. Knowing with what coldness, or, at the best, uncandor, he (representing Society in its attitude toward convicted Error) would have met the fact had it been owned to him at first, he had not virtue enough to condemn the illusory stranger, who must have been helpless to make at once evident any repentance he felt or good purpose he cherished. Was it not one of the saddest consequences of the man's past,—a dark necessity of misdoing,—that, even with the best will in the world to retrieve himself, his first endeavor must involve a wrong? Might he not, indeed, be considered a martyr, in some sort, to his own admirable impulses? I can see clearly enough where the contributor was astray in this reasoning, but I can also understand how one accustomed to value realities only as they resembled fables should be won with such pensive sophistry; and I can certainly sympathize with his feeling that the mariner's failure to reappear according to appointment added its final and most agreeable charm to the whole affair, and completed the mystery from which the man emerged and which swallowed him up again.

SCENE

On that loveliest autumn morning, the swollen tide had spread over all the russet levels, and gleamed in the sunlight a mile away. As the contributor moved onward down the street, luminous on either hand with crimsoning and yellowing maples, he was so filled with the tender serenity of the scene, as not to be troubled by the spectacle of small Irish houses standing miserably about on the flats ankle deep, as it were, in little pools of the tide, or to be aware at first, of a strange stir of people upon the streets: a fluttering to and fro and lively encounter and separation of groups of bareheaded women, a flying of children through the broken fences of the neighborhood, and across the vacant lots on which the insulted sign-boards forbade them to trespass; a sluggish movement of men through all, and a pause of different vehicles along the sidewalks. When a sense of these facts had penetrated his enjoyment, he asked a matron whose snowy arms, freshly taken from the wash-tub, were folded across a mighty chest, "What is the matter?"

"A girl drowned herself, sir-r-r, over there on the flats, last Saturday, and they're looking for her."

"It was the best thing she could do," said another matron grimly.

Upon this answer that literary soul fell at once to patching himself up a romantic story for the suicide, after the pitiful fashion of this fiction-ridden age, when we must relate everything we see to something we have read. He was the less to blame for it, because he could not help it; but certainly he is not to be praised for his associations with the tragic fact brought to his notice. Nothing could have been more trite or obvious, and he felt his intellectual poverty so keenly that he might almost have believed his discomfort a sympathy for the girl who had drowned herself last Saturday. But of course, this could not be, for he had but lately been thinking what a very tiresome figure to the imagination the Fallen Woman had become. As a fact of Christian civilization, she was a spectacle to wring one's heart, he owned; but he wished she were well out of the romances, and it really seemed a fatality that she should be the principal personage of this little scene. The preparation for it, whatever it was to be, was so deliberate, and the reality had so slight relation to the French roofs and modern improvements of the comfortable Charlesbridge which he knew, that he could not consider himself other than as a spectator awaiting some entertainment, with a faint inclination to be critical.

In the mean time there passed through the motley crowd, not so much a cry as a sensation of "They've found her, they've found her!" and then the one terrible picturesque fact, "She was standing upright!"

Upon this there was wilder and wilder clamor among the people, dropping by degrees and almost dying away, before a flight of boys came down the street with the tidings, "They are bringing her—bringing her in a wagon."

The contributor knew that she whom they were bringing in the wagon, had had the poetry of love to her dismal and otherwise squalid death; but the history was of fancy, not of fact in his mind. Of course, he reflected, her lot must have been obscure and hard; the aspect of those concerned about her death implied that. But of her hopes and her fears, who could tell him anything? To be sure he could imagine the lovers, and how they first met, and where, and who he was that was doomed to work her shame and death; but here his fancy came upon something coarse and common: a man of her own race and grade, handsome after that manner of beauty which is so much more hateful than ugliness is; or, worse still, another kind of man whose deceit must have been subtler and wickeder; but whatever the person, a presence defiant of sympathy or even interest, and simply horrible. Then there were the details of the affair, in great degree common to all love affairs, and not varying so widely in any condition of life; for the passion which is so rich and infinite to those within its charm, is apt to seem a little tedious and monotonous in its character, and poor in resources to the cold looker-on.

Then, finally, there was the crazy purpose and its fulfillment: the headlong plunge from bank or bridge; the eddy, and the bubbles on the current that calmed itself above the suicide; the tide that rose and stretched itself abroad in the sunshine, carrying hither and thither the burden with which it knew not what to do; the arrest, as by some ghastly caprice of fate, of the dead girl, in that upright posture, in which she should meet the quest for her, as it were defiantly.

And now they were bringing her in a wagon.

Involuntarily all stood aside, and waited till the funeral car, which they saw, should come up toward them through the long vista of the maple-shaded street, a noiseless riot stirring the legs and arms of the boys into frantic demonstration, while the women remained quiet with arms folded or akimbo. Before and behind the wagon, driven slowly, went a guard of ragged urchins, while on the raised seat above sat two Americans, unperturbed by anything, and concerned merely with the business of the affair.

The vehicle was a grocer's cart which had perhaps been pressed into the service; and inevitably the contributor thought of Zenobia, and of Miles Coverdale's belief that if she could have foreboded all the *post-mortem* ugliness and grotesqueness of suicide, she never would have drowned herself. This girl, too, had doubtless had her own ideas of the effect that her death was to make, her conviction that it was to wring one heart, at least, and to strike awe and pity to every other; and her woman's soul must have been shocked from death could she have known in what a ghastly comedy the body she put off was to play a part.

In the bottom of the cart lay something long and straight and terrible, covered with a red shawl that drooped over the end of the wagon; and on this thing were piled the baskets in which the grocers had delivered their orders for sugar and flour, and coffee and tea. As the cart jolted through their lines, the boys could no longer be restrained; they broke out with wild yells, and danced madly about it, while the red shawl hanging from the rigid feet nodded to their frantic mirth; and the sun dropped its light through the maples and shone bright upon the flooded date.

JUBILEE DAYS

I believe I have no good reason for including among these suburban sketches my recollections of the Peace Jubilee, celebrated by a monster musical entertainment at Boston, in June, 1869; and I do not know if it will serve as excuse for their intrusion to say that the exhibition was not urban in character, and that I attended it in a feeling of curiosity and amusement which the Bostonians did not seem to feel, and which I suspect was a strictly suburban if not rural sentiment.

I thought, on that Tuesday morning, as our horse-car drew near the Long Bridge, and we saw the Coliseum spectral through the rain, that Boston was going to show people representing other parts of the country her Notion of weather. I looked forward to a forenoon of clammy warmth, and an afternoon of clammy cold and of east wind, with a misty nightfall soaking men to the bones. But the day really turned out well enough; it was showery, but not shrewish, and it smiled pleasantly at sunset, as if content with the opening ceremonies of the Great Peace Jubilee.

The city, as we entered it, gave due token of excitement, and we felt the celebration even in the air, which had a holiday quality very different from that of ordinary workday air. The crowds filled the decorous streets, and the trim pathways of the Common and the Public Garden, and flowed in an orderly course towards the vast edifice on the Back Bay, presenting the interesting points which always distinguish a crowd come to town from a city crowd. You get so used to the Boston face and the Boston dress, that a coat from New York or a visage from Chicago is at once conspicuous to you; and in these people there was not only this strangeness, but the different oddities that lurk in out-of-way corners of society everywhere had started suddenly into notice. Long-haired men, popularly supposed to have perished with the institution of slavery, appeared before me, and men with various causes and manias looking from their wild eyes confronted each other, let alone such charlatans as had clothed themselves quaintly or grotesquely to add a charm to the virtue of whatever nostrum they peddled. It was, however, for the most part, a remarkably well-dressed crowd; and therein it probably differed more than in any other respect from the crowd which a holiday would have assembled in former times. There was little rusticity to be noted anywhere, and the uncouthness which has already disappeared from the national face seemed to be passing from the national wardrobe. Nearly all the visitors seemed to be Americans, but neither the Yankee type nor the Hoosier was to be found. They were apparently very happy, too; the ancestral solemnity of the race that amuses itself sadly was not to be seen in them, and, if they were not making it a duty to be gay, they were really taking their pleasure in a cheerful spirit.

There was, in fact, something in the sight of the Coliseum, as we approached it, which was a sufficient cause of elation to whoever is buoyed up by the flutter of bright flags, and the movement in and about holiday booths, as I think we all are apt to be. One may not have the stomach of happier days for the swing or the whirligig; he may not drink soda-water intemperately;

pop-corn may not tempt him, nor tropical fruits allure; but he beholds them without gloom,—nay, a grin inevitably lights up his countenance at the sight of a great show of these amusements and refreshments. And any Bostonian might have felt proud that morning that his city did not hide the light of her mercantile merit under a bushel, but blazoned it about on the booths and walls in every variety of printed and painted advertisement. To the mere aesthetic observer, these vast placards gave the delight of brilliant color, and blended prettily enough in effect with the flags; and at first glance I received quite as much pleasure from the frescoes that advised me where to buy my summer clothing, as from any bunting I saw.

I had the good fortune on the morning of this first Jubilee day to view the interior of the Coliseum when there was scarcely anybody there,—a trifle of ten thousand singers at one end, and a few thousand other people scattered about over the wide expanses of parquet and galleries. The decorations within, as without, were a pleasure to the eyes that love gayety of color; and the interior was certainly magnificent, with those long lines of white and blue drapery roofing the balconies, the slim, lofty columns festooned with flags and drooping banners, the arms of the States decking the fronts of the galleries, and the arabesques of painted muslin everywhere. I do not know that my taste concerned itself with the decorations, or that I have any taste in such things; but I testify that these tints and draperies gave no small part of the comfort of being where all things conspired for one's pleasure. The airy amplitude of the building, the perfect order and the perfect freedom of movement, the ease of access and exit, the completeness of the arrangements that in the afternoon gave all of us thirty thousand spectators a chance to behold the great spectacle as well as to hear the music, were felt, I am sure, as personal favors by every one. These minor particulars, in fact, served greatly to assist you in identifying yourself, when the vast hive swarmed with humanity, and you became a mere sentient atom of the mass.

It was rumored in the morning that the ceremonies were to begin with prayer by a hundred ministers, but I missed this striking feature of the exhibition, for I did not arrive in the afternoon till the last speech was being made by a gentleman whom I saw gesticulating effectively, and whom I suppose to have been intelligible to a matter of twenty thousand people in his vicinity, but who was to me, of the remote, outlying thirty thousand, a voice merely. One word only I caught, and I report it here that posterity may know as much as we thirty thousand contemporaries did of

THE PRESIDENT'S SPEECH.

. . . . *(sensation.)* . . . .
. . . *(cheers.)* . . . . refinement . . . .
. . . *(great applause.)*

I do not know if I shall be able to give an idea of the immensity of this scene; but if such a reader as has the dimensions of the Coliseum accurately fixed in his mind will, in imagination, densely hide all that interminable array of benching in the parquet and the galleries and the slopes at either end of the edifice with human heads, showing here crowns, there occiputs, and yonder faces, he will perhaps have some notion of the spectacle as we beheld it from the northern hill-side. Some thousands of heads nearest were recognizable as attached by the usual neck to the customary human body, but for the rest, we seemed to have entered a world of cherubim. Especially did the multitudinous singers seated far opposite encourage this illusion; and their fluttering fans and handkerchiefs wonderfully mocked the movement of those cravat-like pinions which the fancy attributed to them. They rose or sank at the wave of the director's baton; and still looked like an innumerable flock of cherubs drifting over some slope of Paradise, or settling upon it,—if cherubs *can* settle.

The immensity was quite as striking to the mind as to the eye, and an absolute democracy was appreciable in it. Not only did all artificial distinctions cease, but those of nature were practically obliterated, and you felt for once the full meaning of unanimity. No one was at a disadvantage; one was as wise, as good, as handsome as another. In most public assemblages, the foolish eye roves in search of the vanity of female beauty, and rests upon some lovely visage, or pretty figure; but here it seemed to matter nothing whether ladies were well or ill-looking; and one might have been perfectly ascetic without self-denial. A blue eye or a black,—what of it? A mass of blonde or chestnut hair, this sort of walking-dress or that,—you might note the difference casually in a few hundred around you; but a sense of those myriads of other eyes and chignons and walking-dresses absorbed the impression in an instant, and left a dim, strange sense of loss, as if all women had suddenly become Woman. For the time, one would have been preposterously conceited to have felt his littleness in that crowd; you never thought of yourself in an individual capacity at all. It was as if you were a private in an army, or a very ordinary billow of the sea, feeling the battle or the storm, in a collective sort of way, but unable to distinguish your sensations from those of the mass. If a rafter had fallen and crushed you and your unimportant row of people, you could scarcely have regarded it as a personal calamity, but might have found it disagreeable as a shock to that great body of humanity. Recall, then, how astonished you were to be recognized by some one, and to have your hand shaken in your individual character of Smith. "Smith? My dear

What's-your-name, I am for the present the fifty-thousandth part of an enormous emotion!"

It was as difficult to distribute the various facts of the whole effect, as to identify one's self. I had only a public and general consciousness of the delight given by the harmony of hues in the parquet below; and concerning the orchestra I had at first no distinct impression save of the three hundred and thirty violin-bows held erect like standing wheat at one motion of the director's wand, and then falling as if with the next he swept them down. Afterwards files of men with horns, and other files of men with drums and cymbals, discovered themselves; while far above all, certain laborious figures pumped or ground with incessant obeisance at the apparatus supplying the organ with wind.

What helped, more than anything else, to restore you your dispersed and wandering individuality was the singing of Parepa-Rosa, as she triumphed over the harmonious rivalry of the orchestra. There was something in the generous amplitude and robust cheerfulness of this great artist that accorded well with the ideal of the occasion; she was in herself a great musical festival; and one felt, as she floated down the stage with her far-spreading white draperies, and swept the audience a colossal courtesy, that here was the embodied genius of the Jubilee. I do not trust myself to speak particularly of her singing, for I have the natural modesty of people who know nothing about music, and I have not at command the phraseology of those who pretend to understand it; but I say that her voice filled the whole edifice with delicious melody, that it soothed and composed and utterly enchanted, that, though two hundred violins accompanied her, the greater sweetness of her note prevailed over all, like a mighty will commanding many. What a sublime ovation for her when a hundred thousand hands thundered their acclaim!

W. D. Howells

A victorious general, an accepted lover, a successful young author,—these know a measure of bliss, I dare say; but in one throb, the singer's heart, as it leaps in exultation at the loud delight of her applausive thousands, must out-enjoy them all. Let me lay these poor little artificial flowers of rhetoric at the feet of the divine singer, as a faint token of gratitude and eloquent intention.

When Parepa (or Prepper, as I have heard her name popularly pronounced) had sung, the revived conscious-ness of an individual life rose in rebellion against the oppression of that dominant vastness. In fact, human nature can stand only so much of any one thing. To a certain degree you accept and conceive of facts truthfully, but beyond this a mere fantasticality rules; and having got enough of grandeur, the senses played themselves false. That array of fluttering and tuning people on the southern slope began to look minute, like the myriad heads assembled in the infinitesimal photograph which you view through one of those little half-inch lorgnettes; and you had the satisfaction of knowing that to any lovely infinitesimality yonder you showed no bigger than a carpet-tack. The whole performance now seemed to be worked by those tireless figures pumping at the organ, in obedience to signals from a very alert figure on the platform below. The choral and orchestral thousands sang and piped and played; and at a given point in the *scena* from Verdi, a hundred fairies in red shirts marched down through the sombre mass of puppets and beat upon as many invisible anvils.

This was the stroke of anti-climax; and the droll sound of those anvils, so far above all the voices and instruments in its pitch, thoroughly disillusioned you and restored you finally to your proper entity and proportions. It was the great error of the great Jubilee, and where almost every-thing else was noble and impressive,—where the direction was faultless, and the singing and instrumentation as perfectly controlled as if they were the result of one volition,—this anvil-beating was alone ignoble and discordant,—trivial and huge merely. Not even the artillery accompaniment, in which the cannon were made to pronounce words of two syllables, was so bad.

The dimensions of this sketch bear so little proportion to those of the Jubilee, that I must perforce leave most of its features unnoticed; but I wish to express the sense of enjoyment which prevailed (whenever the anvils were not beaten) over every other feeling, even over wonder. To the ear as to the eye it was a delight, and it was an assured success in the popular affections from the performance of the first piece. For my own part, if one pleasurable sensation, besides that received from Parepa's singing, distinguished itself from the rest, it was that given by the performance of the exquisite Coronation March from Meyerbeer's "Prophet;" but I say this under protest of the pleasure taken in the choral rendering of the "Star-Spangled Banner." Closely allying themselves to these great raptures were the minor joys of wandering freely about from point to point, of receiving fresh sensations from the varying lights and aspects in which the novel scene presented itself with its strange fascinations, and of noting, half consciously, the incessant movement of the crowd as it revealed itself in changing effects of color. Then the gay tumult of the fifteen minutes of intermission between the parts, when all rose with a *susurrus* of innumerable silks, and the thousands of pretty singers fluttered about, and gossiped tremulously and delightedly over the glory of the performance, revealing themselves as charming feminine personalities, each with her share in the difficulty and the achievement, each with her pique or pride, and each her something to tell her friend of the conduct, agreeable or displeasing, of some particular him! Even the quick dispersion of the mass at the close was a marvel of orderliness and grace, as the melting and separating parts, falling asunder, radiated from the centre, and flowed and rippled rapidly away, and left the great hall empty and bare at last.

And as you emerged from the building, what bizarre and perverse feeling was that you knew? Something as if all-out-doors were cramped and small, and it were better to return to the freedom and amplitude of the interior?

On the second day, much that was wonderful in a first experience of the festival was gone; but though the novelty had passed away, the cause for wonder was even greater. If on the first day the crowd was immense, it was now something which the imperfect state of the language will not permit me to describe; perhaps *awful* will serve the purpose as well as any other word now in use. As you looked round, from the centre of the building, on that restless, fanning, fluttering multitude, to right and left and north and south, all comparisons and similitudes abandoned you. If you were to write of the scene, you felt that your effort, at the best, must be a meagre sketch, suggesting something to those who had seen the fact, but conveying no intelligible impression of it to any one else. The galleries swarmed, the vast slopes were packed, in the pampa-like parquet even the aisles were half filled with chairs, while a cloud of placeless wanderers moved ceaselessly on the borders of the mass under the balconies.

When that common-looking, uncommon little man whom we have called to rule over us entered the house, and walked quietly down to his seat in the centre of it, a wild, inarticulate clamor, like no other noise in the world, swelled from every side, till General Grant rose and showed himself, when it grew louder than ever, and then gradually subsided into silence. Then a voice, which might be uttering some mortal alarm, broke repeatedly across the stillness from one of the balconies, and a thousand glasses were leveled in that direction, while everywhere else the mass hushed itself with a mute sense of peril. The capacity of such an assemblage for self-destruction was, in fact, but too evident. From fire, in an edifice of which the sides could be knocked out in a moment, there could have been little danger; the fabric's strength had been perfectly tested the day before, and its fall was not to be apprehended; but we had ourselves greatly to dread. A panic could have been caused by any mad or wanton person, in which thousands might have been instantly trampled to death; and it seemed long till that foolish voice was stilled, and the house lapsed back into tranquillity, and the enjoyment of the music. In the performance I recall nothing disagreeable, nothing that to my ignorance seemed imperfect, though I leave it to the wise in music to say how far the great concert was a success. I saw a flourish of the director's wand, and I heard the voices or the instruments, or both, respond, and I knew by my programme that I was enjoying an unprecedented quantity of Haydn or Handel or Meyerbeer or Rossini or Mozart, afforded with an unquestionable precision and promptness; but I own that I liked better to stroll about the three-acre house, and that for me the music was, at best, only one of the joys of the festival.

There was good hearing outside for those that desired to listen to the music, with seats to let in the surrounding tents and booths; and there was unlimited seeing for the mere looker-on. At least fifty thousand people seemed to have come to the Jubilee with no other purpose than to gaze upon the outside of the building. The crowd was incomparably greater than that of the day before; all the main thoroughfares of the city roared with a tide of feet that swept through the side streets, and swelled aimlessly up the places, and eddied there, and poured out again over the pavements. The carriage-ways were packed with every sort of vehicle, with foot-passengers crowded from the sidewalks, and with the fragments of the military parade in honor of the President, with infantry, with straggling cavalrymen, with artillery. All the paths of the Common and the Garden were filled, and near the Coliseum the throngs densified on every side into an almost impenetrable mass, that made the doors of the building difficult to approach and at times inaccessible.

The crowd differed from that of the first day chiefly in size. There were more country faces and country garbs to be seen, though it was still, on the whole, a regular-featured and well-dressed crowd, with still very few but American visages. It seemed to be also a very frugal-minded crowd, and to spend little upon the refreshments and amusements provided for it. In these, oddly enough, there was nothing of the march of mind to be observed; they Were the refreshments and amusements of a former generation. I think it would not be extravagant to say that there were tons of pie for sale in a multitude of booths, with lemonade, soda-water, and ice-cream in proportion; but I doubt if there was a ton of pie sold, and towards the last the venerable pastry was quite covered with dust. Neither did people seem to care much for oranges or bananas or peanuts, or even pop-corn,—five cents a package and a prize in each package. Many booths stood unlet, and in others the pulverous ladies and gentlemen, their proprietors, were in the enjoyment of a leisure which would have been elegant if it had not been forced. There was one shanty, not otherwise distinguished from the rest, in which French soups were declared to be for sale; but these alien pottages seemed to be no more favored than the most poisonous of our national viands. But perhaps they were not French soups, or perhaps the vicinage of the shanty was not such as to impress a belief in their genuineness upon people who like French soups. Let us not be too easily disheartened by the popular neglect of them. If the daring reformer who inscribed French soups upon his sign will reappear ten years hence, we shall all flock to his standard. Slavery is abolished; pie must follow. Doubtless in the year 1900, the managers of a Jubilee would even let the refreshment-rooms within their Coliseum to a cook who would offer the public something not so much worse than the worst that could be found in the vilest shanty restaurant on the ground. At the Jubilee, of which I am writing, the unhappy person who went into the Coliseum rooms to refresh himself was offered for coffee a salty and unctuous wash, in one of those thick cups which are supposed to be proof against the hard usage of "guests" and scullions in humble eating-houses, and which are always so indescribably nicked and cracked, and had pushed towards him a bowl of veteran sugar, and a tin spoon that had never been cleaned in the world, while a young person stood by, and watched him, asking, "Have you paid for that coffee?"

The side-shows and the other amusements seemed to have addressed themselves to the crowd with the same mistaken notion of its character and requirements; though I confess that I witnessed their neglect with regret, whether from a feeling that they were at least harmless, or an unconscious sympathy with any quite idle and unprofitable thing. Those rotary, legless horses, on which children love to ride in a perpetual sickening circle,—the type of all our effort,—were nearly always mounted; but those other whirligigs, or whatever the dreadful circles with their swinging seats are called, were often so empty that they must have been distressing, from their want of balance, to the muscles as well as the spirits of their proprietors. The society of monsters was also generally shunned, and a cow with five legs gave milk from the top of her back to an audience of not more than six persons. The public apathy had visibly wrought upon the temper of the gentleman who lectured upon this gifted animal, and he took inquiries in an ironical manner that contrasted disadvantageously with the philosophical serenity of the person who had a weighing-machine outside, and whom I saw sitting in the chair and weighing himself by the hour, with an expression of profound enjoyment. Perhaps a man of less bulk could not have entered so keenly into that simple pleasure.

There was a large tent on the grounds for dramatical entertainments, with six performances a day, into which I was lured by a profusion of high-colored posters, and some such announcement, as that the beautiful serio-comic danseuse and world-renowned cloggist, Mile. Brown, would appear. About a dozen people were assembled within, and we waited a half-hour beyond the time announced for the curtain to rise, during which the spectacle of a young man in black broadcloth, eating a cocoa-nut with his pen-knife, had a strange and painful fascination. At the end of this half-hour, our number was increased to eighteen, when the orchestra appeared,—a snare-drummer and two buglers. These took their place at the back of the tent; the buglers, who were Germans, blew seriously and industriously at their horns; but the native-born citizen, who played the drum, beat it very much at random, and in the mean time smoked a cigar, while his humorous friend kept time upon his shoulders by striking him there with a cane. How long this might have lasted, I cannot tell; but, after another delay, I suddenly bethought me whether it were not better not to see Mile. Brown, after all? I rose, and stole softly out behind the rhythmic back of the drummer; and the world-renowned cloggist is to me at this moment only a beautiful dream,—an airy shape fashioned upon a hint supplied by the engraver of the posters.

What, then, did the public desire, if it would not smile

upon the swings, or monsters, or dramatic amusements that had pleased so long? Was the music, as it floated out from the Coliseum, a sufficient delight? Or did the crowd, averse to the shows provided for it, crave something higher and more intellectual,—like, for example, a course of the Lowell Lectures? Its general expression had changed: it had no longer that entire gayety of the first day, but had taken on something of the sarcastic pathos with which we Americans bear most oppressive and fatiguing things as a good joke. The dust was blown about in clouds; and here and there, sitting upon the vacant steps that led up and down among the booths, were dejected and motionless men and women, passively gathering dust, and apparently awaiting burial under the accumulating sand,—the mute, melancholy sphinxes of the Jubilee, with their unsolved riddle, "Why did we come?" At intervals, the heavens shook out fierce, sudden showers of rain, that scattered the surging masses, and sent them flying impotently hither and thither for shelter where no shelter was, only to gather again, and move aimlessly and comfortlessly to and fro, like a lost child.

So the multitude roared within and without the Coliseum as I turned homeward; and yet I found it wandering with weary feet through the Garden, and the Common, and all the streets, and it dragged its innumerable aching legs with me to the railroad station, and, entering the train, stood up on them,—having paid for the tickets with which the companies professed to sell seats.

How still and cool and fresh it was at our suburban station, when the train, speeding away with a sardonic yell over the misery of the passengers yet standing up in it, left us to walk across the quiet fields and pleasant lanes to Benicia Street, through groups of little idyllic Irish boys playing base-ball, with milch-goats here and there pastorally cropping the herbage!

In this pleasant seclusion I let all Bunker Hill Day thunder by, with its cannons, and processions, and speeches, and patriotic musical uproar, hearing only through my open window the note of the birds singing in a leafy coliseum across the street, and making very fair music without an anvil among them. "Ah, signer!" said one of my doorstep acquaintance, who came next morning and played me Captain Jenks,—the new air he has had added to his instrument,—"never in my life, neither at Torino, nor at Milano, nor even at Genoa, never did I see such a crowd or hear such a noise, as at that Colosseo yesterday. The carriages, the horses, the feet! And the dust, O Dio mio! All those millions of people were as white as so many millers!"

On the afternoon of the fourth day the city looked quite like the mill in which these millers had been grinding; and even those unpromisingly elegant streets of the Back Bay showed mansions powdered with dust enough for senti- ment to strike root in, and so soften them with its tender green against the time when they shall be ruinous and sentiment shall swallow them up. The crowd had percep- tibly diminished, but it was still great, and on the Common it was allured by a greater variety of recreations and bargains than I had yet seen there. There were, of course, all sorts of useful and instructive amusements,—at least a half-dozen telescopes, and as many galvanic batteries, with numerous patented inventions; and I fancied that most of the peddlers and charlatans addressed themselves to a utilitarian spirit supposed to exist in us. A man that sold whistles capable of reproducing exactly the notes of the mocking-bird and the guinea-pig set forth the durability of the invention. "Now, you see this whistle, gentlemen. It is rubber, all rubber; and rubber, you know, enters into the composition of a great many valuable articles. This whistle, then, is entirely of rubber,—no worthless or flimsy material that drops to pieces the moment you put it to your lips,"—as if it were not utterly desirable that it should. "Now, I'll give you the mocking-bird, gentlemen, and then I'll give you the guinea-pig, upon this pure *India*-rubber whistle." And he did so with a great animation,—this young man with a perfectly intelligent and very handsome face. "Try your strength, and renovate your system!" cried the proprietor of a piston padded at one end and working into a cylinder when you struck it a blow with your fist; and the owners of lung-testing machines called upon you from every side to try their consumption cure; while the galvanic-battery men sat still and mutely appealed with inscriptions attached to their cap-visors declaring that electricity taken from their batteries would rid you of every ache and pain known to suffering humanity. Yet they were themselves as a class in a state of sad physical disrepair, and one of them was the visible prey of rheumatism which he might have sent flying from his joints with a single shock. The only person whom I saw improving his health with the battery was a rosy-faced school-boy, who was taking ten cents' worth of electricity; and I hope it did not disagree with his pop-corn and soda-water.

Farther on was a picturesque group of street-musicians,— violinists and harpers; a brother and four sisters, by their looks,—who afforded almost the only unpractical amusement to be enjoyed on the Common, though not far from them was a blind old negro, playing upon an accordion, and singing to it in the faintest and thinnest of black voices, who could hardly have profited any listener. No one appeared to mind him, till a jolly Jack-tar with both arms cut off, but dressed in full sailor's togs, lurched heavily towards him. This mariner had got quite a good effect of sea-legs by some means, and looked rather drunker than a man with both arms ought to be; but he was very affectionate, and, putting his face close to the other's, at once entered into talk with the blind man, forming with him a picture curiously pathetic and grotesque. He was the only tipsy person I saw during the Jubilee days,—if he was tipsy, for after all they may have been real sea-legs he had on.

If the throng upon the streets was thinner, it was greater in the Coliseum than on the second day; and matters had settled there into regular working order. The limits of individual liberty had been better ascertained; there was no longer any movement in the aisles, but a constant passing to and fro, between the pieces, in the promenades. The house presented, as before, that appearance in which reality forsook it, and it became merely an amazing picture. The audience supported the notion of its unreality by having exactly the character of the former audiences, and impressed you, despite its restlessness and incessant agitation, with the feeling that it had remained there from the first day, and would always continue there; and it was only in wandering upon its borders through the promenades, that you regained possession of facts concerning it. In no other way was its vastness more observable than in the perfect indifference of persons one to another. Each found himself, as it were, in a solitude; and, sequestered in that wilderness of strangers, each was freed of his bashfulness and trepidation. Young people lounged at ease upon the floors, about the windows, on the upper promenades; and in this seclusion I saw such betrayals of tenderness as melt the heart of the traveller on our desolate railway trains,—Fellows moving to and fro or standing, careless of other eyes, with their arms around the waists of their Girls. These were, of course, people who had only attained a certain grade of civilization, and were not characteristic of the crowd, or, indeed, worthy of notice except as expressions of its unconsciousness. I fancied that I saw a number of their class outside listening to the address of the agent of a patent liniment, proclaimed to be an unfailing specific for neuralgia and headache,—if used in the right spirit. "For," said the orator, "we like to cure people who treat us and our medicine with respect. Folks say, 'What is there about that man?—some magnetism or electricity.' And the other day at New Britain, Connecticut, a young man he come up to the carriage, sneering like, and he tried the cure, and it didn't have the least effect upon him." There seemed reason in this, and it produced a visible sensation in the Fellows and Girls, who grinned sheepishly at each other.

Why will the young man with long hair force himself at this point into a history, which is striving to devote itself to graver interests? There he stood with the other people, gazing up at the gay line of streamers on the summit of the Coliseum, and taking in the Anvil Chorus with the rest,—a young man well-enough dressed, and of a pretty sensible face, with his long black locks falling from under his cylinder hat, and covering his shoulders. What awful spell was on him, obliging him to make that figure before his fellow-creatures? He had nothing to sell; he was not, apparently, an advertisement of any kind. Was he in the performance of a vow? Was he in his right mind? For shame! a person may wear his hair long if he will. But why not, then, in a top-knot? This young man's long hair was not in keeping with his frock-coat and his cylinder hat, and he had not at all the excuse of the old gentleman who sold salve in the costume of Washington's time; one could not take pleasure in him as in the negro advertiser, who paraded the grounds in a costume compounded of a consular *chapeau bras* and a fox-hunter's top-boots—the American diplomatic uniform of the future—and offered every one a printed billet; he had not even the attraction of the cabalistic herald of Hunkidori. Who was he? what was he? why was he? The mind played forever around these questions in a maze of hopeless conjecture.

Had all those quacks and peddlers been bawling ever

since Tuesday to the same listeners? Had all those swings and whirligigs incessantly performed their rounds? The cow that gave milk from the top of her back, had she never changed her small circle of admirers, or ceased her flow? And the gentleman who sat in the chair of his own balance, how much did he weigh by this time? One could scarcely rid one's self of the illusion of perpetuity concerning these things, and I could not believe that, if I went back to the Coliseum grounds at any future time, I should not behold all that vast machinery in motion.

It was curious to see, amid this holiday turmoil men pursuing the ordinary business of their lives, and one was strangely rescued and consoled by the spectacle of the Irish hod-carriers, and the bricklayers at work on a first-class swell-front residence in the very heart of the city of tents and booths. Even the locomotive, being associated with quieter days and scenes, appealed, as it whistled to and fro upon the Providence Railroad, to some soft bucolic sentiment in the listener, and sending its note, ordinarily so discordant, across that human uproar, seemed to "babble of green fields." And at last it wooed us away, and the Jubilee was again swallowed up by night.

There was yet another Jubilee Day, on the morning of which the thousands of public-school children clustered in gauzy pink and white in the place of the mighty chorus, while the Coliseum swarmed once more with people who listened to those shrill, sweet pipes blending in unison; but I leave the reader to imagine what he will about it. A week later, after all was over, I was minded to walk down towards the Coliseum, and behold it in its desertion. The city streets were restored to their wonted summer-afternoon tranquillity; the Public Garden presented its customary phases of two people sitting under a tree and talking intimately together on some theme of common interest,—

"Bees, bees, was it your hydromel?"—

of the swans sailing in full view upon the little lake of half a dozen idlers hanging upon the bridge to look at them; of children gayly dotting the paths here and there; and, to heighten the peacefulness of the effect, a pretty, pale invalid lady sat, half in shade and half in sun, reading in an easy-chair. Far down the broad avenue a single horse-car tinkled slowly; on the steps of one of the mansions charming little girls stood in a picturesque group full of the bright color which abounds in the lovely dresses of this time. As I drew near the Coliseum, I could perceive the desolation which had fallen upon the festival scene; the white tents were gone; the place where the world-renowned cloggist gave her serio-comic dances was as lonely and silent as the site of Carthage; in the middle distance two men were dismantling a motionless whirligig; the hut for the sale of French soups was closed; farther away, a solitary policeman moved gloomily across the deserted spaces, showing his dark-blue figure against the sky. The vast fabric of the Coliseum reared itself, hushed and deserted within and without; and a boy in his shirt-sleeves pressed his nose against one of the painted window-panes in the vain effort to behold the nothing inside. But sadder than this loneliness surrounding the Coliseum, sadder than the festooned and knotted banners that drooped funereally upon its facade, was the fact that some of those luckless refreshment-saloons were still open, displaying viands as little edible now as carnival *confetti*. It was as if the proprietors, in an unavailing remorse, had condemned themselves to spend the rest of their days there, and, slowly consuming their own cake and pop-corn, washed down with their own soda-water and lemonade, to perish of dyspepsia and despair.

SOME LESSONS FROM THE
SCHOOL OF MORALS

Any study of suburban life would be very imperfect without some glance at that larger part of it which is spent in the painful pursuit of pleasures such as are offered at the ordinary places of public amusement; and for this reason I excuse myself for rehearsing certain impressions here which are not more directly suburban, to say the least, than those recounted in the foregoing chapter.

It became, shortly after life in Charlesbridge began, a question whether any entertainment that Boston could offer were worth the trouble of going to it, or, still worse, coming from it; for if it was misery to hurry from tea to catch the inward horse-car at the head of the street, what sullen lexicon will afford a name for the experience of getting home again by the last car out from the city? You have watched the clock much more closely than the stage during the last act, and have left your play incomplete by its final marriage or death, and have rushed up to Bowdoin Square, where you achieve a standing place in the car, and, utterly spent as you are with the enjoyment of the evening, you endure for the next hour all that is horrible in riding or walking. At the end of this time you declare that you will never go to the theatre again; and after years of suffering you come at last to keep your word.

While yet, however, in the state of formation as regards this resolution, I went frequently to the theatre—or school of morals, as its friends have humorously called it. I will not say whether any desired amelioration took place or not in my own morals through the agency of the stage; but if not enlightened and refined by everything I saw there, I sometimes was certainly very much surprised. Now that I go no more, or very, very rarely, I avail myself of the resulting leisure to set down, for the instruction of posterity, some account of performances I witnessed in the years 1868-69, which I am persuaded will grow all the more curious, if not incredible, with the lapse of time.

There is this satisfaction in living, namely, that whatever we do will one day wear an air of picturesqueness and romance, and will win the fancy of people coming after us. This stupid and commonplace present shall yet appear the fascinating past; and is it not a pleasure to think how our rogues of descendants—who are to enjoy us aesthetically—will be taken in with us, when they read, in the files of old newspapers, of the quantity of entertainment offered us at the theatres during the years mentioned, and judge us by it? I imagine them two hundred years hence looking back at us, and sighing, "Ah! there was a touch of the old Greek life in those Athenians! How they loved the drama in the jolly Boston of that day! That was the golden age of the theatre: in the winter of 1868-69, they had dramatic performances in seven places, of every degree of excellence, and the managers coined money." As we always figure our ancestors going to and from church, they will probably figure us thronging the doors of theatres, and no doubt there will be some historical gossiper among them to sketch a Boston audience in 1869, with all our famous poets and politicians grouped together in the orchestra seats, and several now dead introduced with the pleasant inaccuracy and uncertainty of historical gossipers. "On this night, when the beautiful

Tostee reappeared, the whole house rose to greet her. If Mr. Alcott was on one of his winter visits to Boston, no doubt he stepped in from the Marlborough House,—it was a famous temperance hotel, then in the height of its repute,—not only to welcome back the great actress, but to enjoy a chat between the acts with his many friends. Here, doubtless, was seen the broad forehead of Webster; there the courtly Everett, conversing in studied tones with the gifted So-and-so. Did not the lovely Such-a-one grace the evening with her presence? The brilliant and versatile Edmund Kirke was dead; but the humorous Artemas Ward and his friend Nasby may have attracted many eyes, having come hither at the close of their lectures, to testify their love of the beautiful in nature and art; while, perhaps, Mr. Sumner, in the intervals of state cares, relaxed into the enjoyment," etc. "Vous voyez bien le tableau!"

That far-off posterity, learning that all our theatres are filled every night, will never understand but we were a theatre-going people in the sense that it is the highest fashion to be seen at the play; and yet we are sensible that it is not so, and that the Boston which makes itself known in civilization—in letters, politics, reform—goes as little to the theatre as fashionable Boston.

The stage is not an Institution with us, I should say; yet it affords recreation to a very large and increasing number of persons, and while it would be easy to over-estimate its influence for good or evil even with these, there is no doubt that the stage, if not the drama, is popular. Fortunately an inquiry like this into a now waning taste in theatricals concerns the fact rather than the effect of the taste otherwise the task might become indefinitely hard alike for writer and for reader. No one can lay his hand on his heart, and declare that he is the worse for having seen "La Belle Helene," for example, or say more than that it is a thing which ought not to be seen by any one else; yet I suppose there is no one ready to deny that "La Belle Helene" was the motive of those performances that have most pleased the most people during recent years. There was something fascinating in the circumstances and auspices under which the united Irma and Tostee troupes appeared in Boston—*opera bouffe* led gayly forward by *finance bouffe*, and suggesting Erie shares by its watered music and morals; but there is no doubt that Tostee's grand reception was owing mainly to the personal favor which she enjoyed here and which we do not vouchsafe to every one. Ristori did not win it; we did our duty by her, following her carefully with the libretto, and in her most intense effects turning the leaves of a thousand pamphlets with a rustle that must have shattered every delicate nerve in her; but we were always cold to her greatness. It was not for Tostees singing, which was but a little thing in itself; it was not for her beauty, for that was no more than a reminiscence, if it was not always an illusion; was it because she rendered the spirit of M. Offenbach's operas so perfectly, that we liked her so much? "Ah, that movement!" cried an enthusiast, "that swing, that—that—wriggle!" She was undoubtedly a great actress, full of subtle surprises, and with an audacious appearance of unconsciousness in those exigencies where consciousness would summon the police—or should; she was so near, yet so far from, the worst that could be intended; in tones, in gestures, in attitudes, she was to the libretto just as the music was, now making it appear insolently and unjustly coarse, now feebly inadequate in its explicit immodesty.

To see this famous lady in "La Grande Duchesse" or "La Belle Helene" was an experience never to be forgotten, and certainly not to be described. The former opera has undoubtedly its proper and blameless charm. There is something pretty and arch in the notion of the Duchess's falling in love with the impregnably faithful and innocent

Fritz; and the extravagance of the whole, with the satire upon the typical little German court, is delightful. But "La Belle Helene" is a wittier play than "La Grande Duchesse," and it is the vividest expression of the spirit of *opera bouffe*. It is full of such lively mockeries as that of Helen when she gazes upon the picture of Leda and the Swan: "J'aime a me recueiller devant ce tableau de famille! Mon pere, ma mere, les voici tous les deux! O mon pere, tourne vers ton enfant un bec favorable!"—or of Paris when he represses the zeal of Calchas, who desires to present him at once to Helen: "Soit! mais sans lui dire qui je suis;—je desire garder le plus strict incognito, jusq'au moment ou la situation sera favorable a un coup de theatre." But it must be owned that our audiences seemed not to take much pleasure in these and other witticisms, though they obliged Mademoiselle Tostee to sing "Un Mari sage" three times, with all those actions and postures which seem incredible the moment they have ceased. They possibly understood this song no better than the strokes of wit, and encored it merely for the music's sake. The effect was, nevertheless, unfortunate, and calculated to give those French ladies but a bad opinion of our morals. How could they comprehend that the taste was, like themselves, imported, and that its indulgence here did not characterize us? It was only in appearance that, while we did not enjoy the wit we delighted in the coarseness. And how coarse this travesty of the old fable mainly is! That priest Calchas, with his unspeakable snicker his avarice, his infidelity, his hypocrisy, is alone infamy enough to provoke the destruction of a city. Then that scene interrupted by Menelaus! It is indisputably witty, and since all those people are so purely creatures of fable, and dwell so entirely in an unmoral atmosphere, it appears as absurd to blame it as the murders in a pantomime. To be sure there is something about murder, some inherent grace or refinement perhaps, that makes its actual representation upon the stage more tolerable than the most diffident suggestion of adultery. Not that "La Belle Helene" is open to the reproach of over-delicacy in this scene, or any other, for the matter of that, though there is a strain of real poetry in the conception of this whole episode of Helen's intention to pass all Paris's love-making off upon herself for a dream,—poetry such as might have been inspired by a muse that had taken too much nectar. There is excellent character, also, as well as caricature in the drama; not only Calchas is admirably done, but Agamemnon, and Achilles, and Helen, and Menelaus, "pas un mari ordinaire ... un mari epique,"—and the burlesque is good of its kind. It is artistic, as it seems French dramatic effort must almost necessarily be. It could scarcely be called the fault of the *opera bouffe* that the English burlesque should have come of its success; nor could the public blame it for the great favor the burlesque won in those far-off winters, if indeed the public wishes to bestow blame for this. No one, however, could see one of these curious travesties without being reminded, in an awkward way, of the *morale* of the *opera bouffe*, and of the *personnel*—as I may say—of "The Black Crook," "The White Fawn," and the "Devil's Auction." There was the same intention of merriment at the cost of what may be called the marital prejudices, though it cannot be claimed that the wit was the same as in "La Belle Helene;" there was the same physical unreserve as in the ballets of a former season; while in its dramatic form the burlesque discovered very marked parental traits.

This English burlesque, this child of M. Offenbach's genius, and the now somewhat faded spectacular muse, flourished at the time of which I write in three of our seven theatres for months,—five, from the highest to the lowest being in turn open to it,—and had begun, in a tentative way, to invade the deserted stage even so long ago as the previous summer; and I have sometimes flattered myself that it was my fortune to witness the first exhibition of its most characteristic feature in a theatre into which I wandered one sultry night because it was the nearest theatre. They were giving a play called "The Three Fast Men," which had a moral of such powerful virtue that it ought to have reformed everybody in the neighborhood. Three ladies being in love with the three fast men, and resolved to win them back to regular hours and the paths of sobriety by every device of the female heart, dress themselves in men's clothes,—such is the subtlety of the female heart in the bosoms of modern young ladies of fashion,—and follow their lovers about from one haunt of dissipation to another and become themselves exemplarily vicious,—drunkards, gamblers, and the like. The first lady, who was a star in her lowly orbit, was very great in all her different *roles*, appearing now as a sailor with the hornpipe of his calling, now as an organ-grinder, and now as a dissolute young gentle-man,—whatever was the exigency of good morals. The dramatist seemed to have had an eye to her peculiar capabilities, and to have expressly invented edifying characters and situations that her talents might enforce them. The second young lady had also a personal didactic gift, rivaling, and even surpassing in some respects, that of the star; and was very rowdy indeed. In due time the devoted conduct of the young ladies has its just effect: the three fast men begin to reflect upon the folly of their wild courses; and at this point the dramatist delivers his great stroke. The first lady gives a *soiree dansante et chantante*, and the three fast men have invitations. The guests seat themselves, as at a fashionable party, in a semicircle, and the gayety of the evening begins with conundrums and playing upon the banjo; the gentlemen are in their morning-coats, and the ladies in a display of hosiery which is now no longer surprising, and which need not have been mentioned at all except for the fact that, in the case of the first lady, it seemed not to have been freshly put on for that party. In this instance an element comical beyond intention was present, in three young gentlemen, an amateur musical trio, who had kindly consented to sing their favorite song of "The Rolling Zuyder Zee," as they now kindly did, with flushed faces, unmanageable hands, and much repetition of

The ro-o-o-o-
The ro-o-o-o-
The ro-o-o-o-ll-
Ing Zuyder Zee,
Zuyder Zee,
Zuyder Zee-e-e!

Then the turn of the three guardian angels of the fast men being come again they get up and dance each one a breakdown which seems to establish their lovers (now at last in the secret of the generous ruse played upon them) firmly in their resolution to lead a better life. They are in nowise shaken from it by the displeasure which soon shows itself in the manner of the first and second ladies. The former is greatest in the so-called Protean parts of the play, and is obscured somewhat by the dancing of the latter; but she has a daughter who now comes on and sings a song. The pensive occasion, the favorable mood of the audience, the sympathetic attitude of the players, invite her to sing "The Maiden's Prayer," and so we have "The Maiden's Prayer." We may be a low set, and the song may be affected and insipid enough, but the purity of its intention touches, and the little girl is vehemently applauded. She is such a pretty child with her innocent face, and her artless white dress, and blue ribbons to her waist and hair, that we will have her back again; where-upon she runs out upon the stage, strikes up a rowdy, rowdy air, dances a shocking little dance, and vanishes from the dismayed vision, leaving us a considerably lower set than we were at first, and glad of our lowness. This is the second lady's own ground, however, and now she comes out—in a way that banishes far from our fickle minds all thoughts of the first lady and her mistaken child—with a medley of singing and dancing, a bit of breakdown, of cancan, of jig, a bit of "Le Sabre de mon Pere," and of all memorable slang songs, given with the most grotesque and clownish spirit that ever inspired a woman. Each member of the company follows in his or her *pas seul*, and then they all dance together to the plain confusion of the amateur trio, whose eyes roll like so many Zuyder Zees, as they sit lonely and motionless in the midst. All stiffness and formality are overcome. The evening party in fact disappears entirely, and we are suffered to see the artists in their moments of social relaxation sitting as it were around the theatrical fireside. They appear to forget us altogether; they exchange winks, and nods, and jests of quite personal application; they call each other by name, by their Christian names, their nicknames. It is not an evening party, it is a family party, and the suggestion of home enjoyment completes the reformation of the three fast men. We see them marry the three fast women before we leave the house.

On another occasion, two suburban friends of the drama beheld a more explicit precursor of the coming burlesque at one of the minor theatres last summer. The great actress whom they had come to see on another scene was ill, and in their disappointment they embraced the hope of entertainment offered them at the smaller playhouse. The drama itself was neither here nor there as to intent, but the public appetite or the manager's conception of it—for I am by no means sure that this whole business was not a misunderstanding—had exacted that the actresses should appear in so much stocking, and so little else, that it was a horror to look upon them. There was no such exigency of dialogue, situation, or character as asked the indecorum, and the effect upon the unprepared spectator was all the more stupefying from the fact that most of the ladies were not dancers, and had not countenances that consorted with impropriety. Their faces had merely the conventional Yankee sharpness and wanness of feature, and such difference of air and character as should say for one and another, shop-girl, shoe-binder, seamstress; and it seemed an absurdity and an injustice to refer to them in any way the disclosures of the ruthlessly scant drapery. A grotesque fancy would sport with their identity: "Did not this or that one write poetry for her local newspaper?" so much she looked the average culture and crudeness, and when such a one, coldly yielding to the manager's ideas of the public taste, stretched herself on a green baize bank with her feet towards us, or did a similar grossness, it was hard to keep from crying aloud in protest, that she need not do it; that nobody really expected or wanted it of her. Nobody? Alas! there were people there—poor souls who had the appearance of coming every night—who plainly did expect it, and who were loud in their applauses of the chief actress. This was a young person of a powerful physical expression, quite unlike the rest,—who were dyspeptic and consumptive in the range of their charms,—and she triumphed and wantoned through the scenes with a fierce excess of animal vigor. She was all stocking, as one may say, being habited to represent a prince; she had a raucous voice, an insolent twist of the mouth, and a terrible trick of defying her enemies by standing erect, chin up, hand on hip, and right foot advanced, patting the floor. It was impossible, even in the orchestra seats, to look at her in this attitude and not shrink before her; and on the stage she visibly tyrannized over the invalid sisterhood with her full-blown fascinations. These unhappy girls personated, with a pathetic effect not to be described, such arch and fantastic creations of the poet's mind as Bewitchingcreature and Exquisitelittlepet, and the play was a kind of fairy burlesque in rhyme, of the most melancholy stupidity that ever was. Yet there was something very comical in the conditions of its performance, and in the possibility that public and manager were playing at cross-purposes. There we were in the pit, an assemblage of hard-working Yankees of decently moral lives and simple traditions, country-bred many of us and of plebeian stock and training, vulgar enough perhaps, but probably not depraved, and, excepting the first lady's friends, certainly not educated to the critical enjoyment of such spectacles; and there on the stage were those mistaken women, in such sad variety of boniness and flabbiness as I have tried to hint, addressing their pitiable exposure to a supposed vileness in us, and wrenching from all original intent the innocent dullness of the drama, which for the most part could have been as well played in walking-dresses, to say the least.

The scene was not less amusing, as regarded the audiences, the ensuing winter, when the English burlesque troupes which London sent us, arrived; but it was not quite so pathetic as regarded the performers. Of their beauty and their abandon, the historical gossiper, whom I descry far down the future, waiting to refer to me as "A scandalous writer of the period," shall learn very little to his purpose of warming his sketch with a color from mine. But I hope I may describe these ladies as very pretty, very blonde, and very unscrupulously clever, and still disappoint the historical gossiper. They seemed in all cases to be English; no Yankee faces, voices, or accents were to be detected among them. Where they were associated with people of another race, as happened with one troupe, the advantage of beauty was upon the Anglo-Saxon side, while that of some small shreds of propriety was with the Latins. These appeared at times almost modest, perhaps because they were the conventional *ballerine*, and wore the old-fashioned ballet-skirt with its volumed gauze,—a coyness which the Englishry had greatly modified, through an exigency of the burlesque,—perhaps because indecorum seems, like blasphemy and untruth, somehow more graceful and becoming in southern than in northern races.

As for the burlesques themselves, they were nothing, the performers personally everything. M. Offenbach had opened Lempriere's Dictionary to the authors with "La Belle Helene," and there, was commonly a flimsy raveling of parodied myth, that held together the different dances and songs, though sometimes it was a novel or an opera burlesqued; but there was always a song and always a dance for each lady, song and dance being equally slangy, and depending for their effect mainly upon the natural or simulated personal charms of the performer.

It was also an indispensable condition of the burlesque's success, that the characters should be reversed in their representation,—that the men's *roles* should be played by women, and that at least one female part should be done by a man. It must be owned that the fun all came from this character, the ladies being too much occupied with the more serious business of bewitching us with their pretty figures to be very amusing; whereas this whole-some man and brother, with his blonde wig, his *panier*, his dainty feminine simperings and languishings, his falsetto tones, and his general air of extreme fashion, was always exceedingly droll. He was the saving grace of these stupid plays; and I cannot help thinking that the *cancan*, as danced, in "Ivanhoe," by Isaac of York and the masculine Rebecca, was a moral spectacle; it was the *cancan* made forever absurd and harmless. But otherwise, the burlesques were as little cheerful as profitable. The playwrights who had adapted them to the American stage—for they were all of English authorship—had been good enough to throw in some political allusions which were supposed to be effective with us, but which it was sad to see received with apathy. It was conceivable from a certain air with which the actors delivered these, that they were in the habit of stirring London audiences greatly with like strokes of satire; but except where Rebecca offered a bottle of Medford rum to Cedric the Saxon, who appeared in the figure of ex-President Johnson, they had no effect upon us. We were cold, very cold, to suggestions of Mr. Reverdy Johnson's now historical speech-making and dining; General Butler's spoons moved us just a little; at the name of Grant we roared and stamped, of course, though in a perfectly mechanical fashion, and without thought of any meaning offered us; those lovely women might have coupled the hero's name with whatever insult they chose, and still his name would have made us cheer them. We seemed not to care for points that were intended to flatter us nationally. I am not aware that anybody signified consciousness when the burlesque supported our side of the Alabama controversy, or acknowledged the self-devotion with which a threat that England should be made to pay was delivered by these English performers. With an equal impassiveness we greeted allusions to Erie shares and to the late Mr. Fiske.

The burlesque chiefly betrayed its descent from the spectacular ballet in its undressing; but that ballet, while it demanded personal exposure, had something very observable in its scenic splendors, and all that marching and processioning in it was rather pretty; while in the burlesque there seemed nothing of innocent intent. No matter what the plot, it led always to a final great scene of breakdown,—which was doubtless most impressive in that particular burlesque where this scene represented the infernal world, and the ladies gave the dances of the country with a happy conception of the deportment of lost souls. There, after some vague and inconsequent dialogue, the wit springing from a perennial source of humor (not to specify the violation of the seventh commandment), the dancing commenced, each performer beginning with the Walk-round of the negro minstrels, rendering its grotesqueness with a wonderful frankness of movement, and then plunging into the mysteries of her dance with a kind of infuriate grace and a fierce delight very curious to look upon. I am aware of the historical gossiper still on the alert for me, and I dare not say how sketchily these ladies were dressed or indeed, more than that they were dressed to resemble circus-riders of the other sex, but as to their own deceived nobody,—possibly did not intend deceit. One of them was so good a player that it seemed needless for her to go so far as she did in the dance; but she spared herself nothing, and it remained for her merely stalwart friends to surpass her, if possible. This inspired each who succeeded her to wantoner excesses, to wilder insolences of hose, to fiercer bravadoes of corsage; while those not dancing responded to the sentiment of the music by singing shrill glees in tune with it, clapping their hands, and patting Juba, as the act is called,—a peculiarly graceful and modest thing in woman. The frenzy grew with every moment, and, as in another Vision of Sin,—

"Then they started from their places,
Moved with violence, changed in hue,
Caught each other with wild grimaces,
Half-invisible to the view,
Wheeling with precipitate paces
To the melody, till they flew,
Hair, and eyes, and limbs, and faces
Twisted hard in fierce embraces,
Like to Furies, like to Graces,"—

with an occasional exchange of cuffs and kicks perfectly human. The spectator found now himself and now the scene incredible, and indeed they were hardly conceivable in relation to each other. A melancholy sense of the absurdity, of the incongruity, of the whole absorbed at last even a sense of the indecency. The audience was much the same in appearance as other audiences, witnessing like displays at the other theatres, and did not differ greatly from the usual theatrical house. Not so much fashion smiled upon the efforts of these young ladies, as upon the *cancan* of the Signorina Morlacchi a winter earlier; but there was a most fair appearance of honest-looking, handsomely dressed men and women; and you could pick out, all over the parquet, faces of one descent from the deaconship, which you wondered were not afraid to behold one another there. The truth is, we spectators, like the performers themselves, lacked that tradition of error, of transgression, which casts its romance about the people of a lighter race. We had not yet set off one corner of the Common for a Jardin Mabille; we had not even the concert-cellars of the gay and elegant New Yorker; and nothing, really, had happened in Boston to educate us to this new taste in theatricals, since the fair Quakers felt moved to testify in the streets and churches against our spiritual nakedness. Yet it was to be noted with regret that our innocence, our respectability, had no restraining influence upon the performance; and the fatuity of the hope cherished by some courageous people, that the presence of virtuous persons would reform the stage, was but too painfully evident. The doubt whether they were not nearer right who have denounced the theatre as essentially and incorrigibly bad would force itself upon the mind, though there was a little comfort in the thought that, if virtue had been actually allowed to frown upon these burlesques, the burlesques might have been abashed into propriety. The caressing arm of the law was cast very tenderly about the performers, and in the only case where a spectator presumed to hiss,—it was at a *pas seul* of the indescribable,—a policeman descended upon him, and with the succor of two friends of the free ballet, rent him from his place, and triumphed forth with him. Here was an end of ungenial criticism; we all applauded zealously after that.

The peculiar character of the drama to which they devoted themselves had produced, in these ladies, some effects doubtless more interesting than profitable to observe. One of them, whose unhappiness it was to take the part of *soubrette* in the Laughable Commedietta preceding the burlesque, was so ill at ease in drapery, so full of awkward jerks and twitches, that she seemed quite another being when she came on later as a radiant young gentleman in pink silk hose, and nothing of feminine modesty in her dress excepting the very low corsage. A strange and compassionable satisfaction beamed from her face; it was evident that this sad business was the poor thing's *forte*. In another company was a lady who had conquered all the easy attitudes of young men of the second or third fashion, and who must have been at something of a loss to identify herself when personating a woman off the stage. But Nature asserted herself in a way that gave a curious and scarcely explicable shock in the case of that dancer whose impudent song required the action of fondling a child, and who rendered the passage with an instinctive tenderness and grace, all the more pathetic for the profaning boldness of her super masculine dress or undress. Commonly, however, the members of these burlesque troupes, though they were not like men, were in most things as unlike women, and seemed creatures of a kind of alien sex, parodying both. It was certainly a shocking thing to look at them with their horrible prettiness, their archness in which was no charm, their grace which put to shame. Yet whoever beheld these burlesque sisters, must have fallen into perplexing question in his own mind as to whose was the wrong involved. It was not the fault of the public—all of us felt that: was it the fault of the hard-working sisterhood, bred to this as to any other business, and not necessarily conscious of the indecorum which pains my reader,—obliged to please somehow, and aiming, doubtless, at nothing but applause? "La Belle Helene" suggests the only reasonable explanation: *"C'est la fatalite."*

FLITTING

I would not willingly repose upon the friendship of a man whose local attachments are weak. I should not demand of my intimate that he have a yearning for the homes of his ancestors, or even the scenes of his own boyhood; that is not in American nature; on the contrary, he is but a poor creature who does not hate the village where he was born; yet a sentiment for the place where one has lived two or three years, the hotel where one has spent a week, the sleeping car in which one has ridden from Albany to Buffalo,—so much I should think it well to exact from my friend in proof of that sensibility and constancy without which true friendship does not exist. So much I am ready to yield on my own part to a friend's demand, and I profess to have all the possible regrets for Benicia Street, now I have left it. Over its deficiencies I cast a veil of decent oblivion, and shall always try to look upon its worthy and consoling aspects, which were far the more numerous. It was never otherwise, I imagine, than an ideal region in very great measure; and if the reader whom I have sometimes seemed to direct thither, should seek it out, he would hardly find my Benicia Street by the city sign-board. Yet this is not wholly because it was an ideal locality, but because much of its reality has now become merely historical, a portion of the tragical poetry of the past. Many of the vacant lots abutting upon Benicia and the intersecting streets flourished up, during the four years we knew it, into fresh-painted wooden houses, and the time came to be when one might have looked in vain for the abandoned hoop-skirts which used to decorate the desirable building-sites. The lessening pasturage also reduced the herds which formerly fed in the vicinity, and at last we caught the tinkle of the cow-bells only as the cattle were driven past to remoter meadows. And one autumn afternoon two laborers, hired by the city, came and threw up an earthwork on the opposite side of the street, which they said was a sidewalk, and would add to the value of property in the neighborhood. Not being dressed with coal-ashes, however, during the winter, the sidewalk vanished next summer under a growth of rag-weed, and hid the increased values with it, and it is now an even question whether this monument of municipal grandeur will finally be held by Art or resumed by Nature,—who indeed has a perpetual motherly longing for her own, and may be seen in all outlying and suburban places, pathetically striving to steal back any neglected bits of ground and conceal them under her skirts of tattered and shabby verdure. But whatever is the event of this contest, and whatever the other changes wrought in the locality, it has not yet been quite stripped of the characteristic charms which first took our hearts, and which have been duly celebrated in these pages.

When the new house was chosen, we made preparations to leave the old one, but preparations so gradual, that, if we had cared much more than we did, we might have suffered greatly by the prolongation of the agony. We proposed to ourselves to escape the miseries of moving by transferring the contents of one room at a time, and if we did not laugh incredulously at people who said we had better have it over at once and be done with it, it was because we respected their feelings, and not because we believed them. We took up one carpet after another; one wall after another we stripped of its pictures; we sent away all the books to begin with; and by this subtle and ingenious process, we reduced ourselves to the discomfort of living in no house at all, as it were, and of being at home in neither one place nor the other. Yet the logic of our scheme remained perfect; and I do not regret its failure in practice, for if we had been ever so loath to quit the old house, its inhospitable barrenness would finally have hurried us forth. In fact, does not life itself in some such fashion dismantle its tenement until it is at last forced out of the uninhabitable place? Are not the poor little comforts and pleasures and ornaments removed one by one, till life, if it would be saved, must go too? We took a lesson from the teachings of mortality, which are so rarely heeded, and we lingered over our moving. We made the process so gradual, indeed, that I do not feel myself all gone yet from the familiar work-room, and for aught I can say, I still write there; and as to the guest-chamber, it is so densely peopled by those it has lodged that it will never quite be emptied of them. Friends also are yet in the habit of calling in the parlor, and talking with us; and will the children never come off the stairs? Does life, our high exemplar, leave so much behind as we did? Is this what fills the world with ghosts?

In the getting ready to go, nothing hurt half so much as the sight of the little girl packing her doll's things for removal. The trousseaux of all those elegant creatures, the wooden, the waxen, the biscuit, the india-rubber, were carefully assorted, and arranged in various small drawers and boxes; their house was thoughtfully put in order and locked for transportation; their innumerable broken sets of dishes were packed in paper and set out upon the floor, a heart-breaking little basketful. Nothing real in this world is so affecting as some image of reality, and this travesty of our own flitting was almost intolerable. I will not pretend to sentiment about anything else, for everything else had in it the element of self-support belonging to all actual afflictions. When the day of moving finally came, and the furniture wagon, which ought to have been only a shade less dreadful to us than a hearse, drew up at our door, our hearts were of a Neronian hardness.

"Were I Diogenes," says wrathful Charles Lamb in one of his letters, "I would not move out of a kilderkin into a hogshead, though the first had nothing but small beer in it, and the second reeked claret." I fancy this loathing of the transitionary state came in great part from the rude and elemental nature of the means of moving in Lamb's day. In our own time, in Charlesbridge at least, everything is so perfectly contrived, that it is in some ways a pleasant excitement to move; though I do not commend the diversion to any but people of entire leisure, for it cannot be denied that it is, at any rate, an interruption to work. But little is broken, little is defaced, nothing is heedlessly outraged or put to shame. Of course there are in every house certain objects of comfort and even ornament which in a state of repose derive a sort of dignity from being cracked, or scratched, or organically debilitated, and give an idea of ancestral possession and of long descent to the actual owner; and you must not hope that this venerable quality will survive their public exposure upon the furniture wagon. There it instantly perishes, like the consequence of some country notable huddled and hustled about in the graceless and ignorant tumult of a great city. To tell the truth, the number of things that turn shabby under the ordeal of moving strikes a pang of unaccustomed poverty to the heart which, loving all manner of makeshifts, is rich even in its dilapidations. For the time you feel degraded by the spectacle of that forlornness, and if you are a man of spirit, you try to sneak out of association with it in the mind of the passer-by; you keep scrupulously in-doors, or if a fancied exigency obliges you to go back and forth between the old house and the new, you seek obscure by-ways remote from the great street down which the wagon flaunts your ruin and decay, and time your arrivals and departures so as to have the air of merely dropping in at either place. This consoles you; but it deceives no one; for the man who is moving is unmistakably stamped with transition.

Yet the momentary eclipse of these things is not the worst. It *is* momentary; for if you will but plant them in kindly corners and favorable exposures of the new house, a mould of respectability will gradually overspread them again, and they will once more account for their presence by the air of having been a long time in the family; but there is danger that in the first moments of mortification you will be tempted to replace them with new and costly articles. Even the best of the old things are nothing to boast of in the hard, unpitying light to which they are exposed, and a difficult and indocile spirit of extravagance is evoked in the least profuse. Because of this fact alone I should not commend the diversion of moving save to people of very ample means as well as perfect leisure; there are more reasons than the misery of flitting why the dweller in the kilderkin should not covet the hogshead reeking of claret.

But the grosser misery of moving is, as I have hinted, vastly mitigated by modern science, and what remains of it one may use himself to with no tremendous effort. I have found that in the dentist's chair,—that ironically luxurious seat, cushioned in satirical suggestion of impossible repose,—after a certain initial period of clawing, filing, scraping, and punching, one's nerves accommodate themselves to the torment, and one takes almost an objective interest in the operation of tooth-filling; and in like manner after two or three wagon-loads of your household stuff have passed down the public street, and all your morbid associations with them have been desecrated, you begin almost to like it. Yet I cannot regard this abandon as a perfectly healthy emotion, and I do not counsel my reader to mount himself upon the wagon and ride to and fro even once, for afterwards the remembrance of such an excess will grieve him.

Of course, I meant to imply by this that moving sometimes comes to an end, though it is not easy to believe so while moving. The time really arrives when you sit down in your new house, and amid whatever disorder take your first meal there. This meal is pretty sure to be that gloomy tea, that loathly repast of butter and toast, and some kind of cake, with which the soul of the early-dining American is daily cast down between the hours of six and seven in the evening; and instinctively you compare it with the last meal you took in your old house, seeking in vain to decide whether this is more dispiriting than that. At any rate that was not at all the meal which the last meal in any house which has been a home ought to be in fact, and is in books. It was hurriedly cooked; it was served upon fugitive and irregular crockery; and it was eaten in deplorable disorder, with the professional movers waiting for the table outside the dining-room. It ought to have been an act of serious devotion; it was nothing but an expiation. It should have been a solemn commemoration of all past dinners in the place, an invocation to their pleasant apparitions. But I, for my part, could not recall these at all, though now I think of them with the requisite pathos, and I know they were perfectly worthy of remembrance. I salute mournfully the companies that have sat down at dinner there, for they are sadly scattered now; some beyond seas, some beyond the narrow gulf, so impassably deeper to our longing and tenderness than the seas. But more sadly still I hail the host himself, and desire to know of him if literature was not somehow a gayer science in those days, and if his peculiar kind of drolling had not rather more heart in it then. In an odd, not quite expressible fashion, something of him seems dispersed abroad and perished in the guests he loved. I trust, of course, that all will be restored to him when he turns—as every man past thirty feels he may when he likes, and has the time—and resumes his youth. Or if this feeling is only a part of the great tacit promise of eternity, I am all the more certain of his getting back his losses.

I say that now these apposite reflections occur to me with a sufficient ease, but that upon the true occasion for them they were absent. So, too, at the first meal in the new house, there was none of that desirable sense of setting up a family altar, but a calamitous impression of irretrievable upheaval, in honor of which sackcloth and ashes seemed the only wear. Yet even the next day the Lares and Penates had regained something of their wonted cheerfulness, and life had begun again with the first breakfast. In fact, I found myself already so firmly established that, meeting the furniture cart which had moved me the day before, I had the face to ask the driver whom they were turning out of house and home, as if my own flitting were a memory of the far-off past.

Not that I think the professional mover expects to be addressed in a joking mood. I have a fancy that he cultivates a serious spirit himself, in which he finds it easy to sympathize with any melancholy on the part of the moving family. There is a slight flavor of undertaking in his manner, which is nevertheless full of a subdued firmness very consoling and supporting; though the life that he leads must be a troubled and uncheerful one, trying alike to the muscles and the nerves. How often must he have been charged by anxious and fluttered ladies to be very careful of that basket of china, and those vases! How often must he have been vexed by the ignorant terrors of gentlemen asking if he thinks that the library-table, poised upon the top of his load, will hold! His planning is not infallible, and when he breaks something uncommonly precious, what does a man of his sensibility do? Is the demolition of old homes really distressing to him, or is he inwardly buoyed up by hopes of other and better homes for the people he moves? Can there be any ideal of moving? Does he, perhaps, feel a pride in an artfully constructed load, and has he something like an artist's pang in unloading it? Is there a choice in families to be moved, and are some worse or better than others? Next to the lawyer and the doctor, it appears to me that the professional mover holds the most confidential relations towards his fellow-men. He is let into all manner of little domestic secrets and subterfuges; I dare say he knows where half the people in town keep their skeleton, and what manner of skeleton it is. As for me, when I saw him making towards a certain closet door, I planted myself firmly against it. He smiled intelligence; he knew the skeleton was there, and that it would be carried to the new house after dark.

I began by saying that I should wish my friend to have some sort of local attachment; but I suppose it must be owned that this sentiment, like pity, and the modern love-passion, is a thing so largely produced by culture that nature seems to have little or nothing to do with it. The first men were homeless wanderers; the patriarchs dwelt in tents, and shifted their place to follow the pasturage, without a sigh; and for children—the pre-historic, the antique people, of our day—moving is a rapture. The last dinner in the old house, the first tea in the new, so doleful to their elders, are partaken of by them with joyous riot. Their shrill trebles echo gleefully from the naked walls and floors; they race up and down the carpetless stairs; they menace the dislocated mirrors and crockery; through all the chambers of desolation they frolic with a gayety indomitable save by bodily exhaustion. If the reader is of a moving family,—and so he is as he is an American,—he can recall the zest he found during childhood in the moving which had for his elders—poor victims of a factitious and conventional sentiment!—only the salt and bitterness of tears. His spirits never fell till the carpets were down; no sorrow touched him till order returned; if Heaven so blessed him that his bed was made upon the floor for one night, the angels visited his dreams. Why, then, is the mature soul, however sincere and humble, not only grieved but mortified by flitting? Why cannot one move without feeling the great public eye fixed in pitying contempt upon him? This sense of abasement seems to be something quite inseparable from the act, which is often laudable, and in every way wise and desirable; and he whom it has afflicted is the first to turn, after his own establishment, and look with scornful compassion upon the overflowing furniture wagon as it passes. But I imagine that Abraham's neighbors, when he struck his tent, and packed his parlor and kitchen furniture upon his camels, and started off with Mrs. Sarah to seek a new camping-ground, did not smile at the procession, or find it worthy of ridicule or lament. Nor did Abraham, once settled, and reposing in the cool of the evening at the door of his tent, gaze sarcastically upon the moving of any of his brother patriarchs.

To some such philosophical serenity we shall also return, I suppose, when we have wisely theorized life in our climate, and shall all have become nomads once more, following June and October up and down and across the continent, and not suffering the full malice of the winter and summer anywhere. But as yet, the derision that attaches to moving attends even the goer-out of town, and the man of many trunks and a retinue of linen-suited womankind is a pitiable and despicable object to all the other passengers at the railroad station and on the steamboat wharf.

This is but one of many ways in which mere tradition

W. D. Howells

oppresses us. I protest that as moving is now managed in Charlesbridge, there is hardly any reason why the master or mistress of the household should put hand to anything; but it is a tradition that they shall dress themselves in their worst, as for heavy work, and shall go about very shabby for at least a day before and a day after the transition. It is a kind of sacrifice, I suppose, to a venerable ideal; and I would never be the first to omit it. In others I observe that this vacant and ceremonious zeal is in proportion to an incapacity to do anything that happens really to be required; and I believe that the truly sage person would devote moving-day to paying visits of ceremony in his finest clothes.

As to the house which one has left, I think it would be preferable to have it occupied as soon as possible after one's flitting. Pilgrimages to the dismantled shrine are certainly to be avoided by the friend of cheerfulness. A day's absence and emptiness wholly change its character, though the familiarity continues, with a ghastly difference, as in the beloved face that the life has left. It is not at all the vacant house it was when you came first to look at it: for then hopes peopled it, and now memories. In that golden prime you had long been boarding, and any place in which you could keep house seemed utterly desirable. How distinctly you recall that wet day, or that fair day, on which you went through it and decided that this should be the guest chamber and that the family room, and what could be done with the little back attic in a pinch! The children could play in the dining-room; and to be sure the parlor was rather small if you wanted to have company; but then, who would ever want to give a party? and besides, the pump in the kitchen was a compensation for anything. How lightly the dumb waiter ran up and down,—

"Qual piuma al vento!"

you sang, in very glad-heartedness. Then estimates of the number of yards of carpeting; and how you could easily save the cost from the difference between boarding and house-keeping. Adieu, Mrs. Brown! henceforth let your "desirable apartments, *en suite* or single, furnished or unfurnished, to gentlemen only!"—this married pair is about to escape forever from your extortions.

Well, if the years passed without making us sadder, should we be much the wiser for their going? Now you know, little couple, that there are extortions in this wicked world beside Mrs. Brown's; and some other things. But if you go into the empty house that was lately your home, you will not, I believe, be haunted by these sordid disappointments, for the place should evoke other regrets and meditations. Truly, though the great fear has not come upon you here, in this room you may have known moments when it seemed very near, and when the quick, fevered breathings of the little one timed your own heart-beats. To that door, with many other missives of joy and pain, came haply the dispatch which hurried you off to face your greatest sorrow—came by night, like a voice of God, speaking and warning, and making all your work idle and your aims foolish. These walls have answered, how many times, to your laughter; they have had friendly ears for the trouble that seemed to grow by utterance. You have sat upon the threshold so many summer days; so many winter mornings you have seen the snows drifted high about it; so often your step has been light and heavy upon it. There is the study, where your magnificent performances were planned, and your exceeding small performances were achieved; hither you hurried with the first criticism of your first book, and read it with the rapture that nothing but a love-letter and a favorable review can awaken. Out there is the well-known humble prospect, that was commonly but a vista into dreamland; on the other hand is the pretty grove,—its leaves now a little painted with the autumn, and faltering to their fall.

Yes, the place must always be sacred, but painfully sacred; and I say again one should not go near it unless as a penance. If the reader will suffer me the confidence, I will own that there is always a pang in the past which is more than any pleasure it can give, and I believe that he, if he were perfectly honest,—as Heaven forbid I or any one should be,—would also confess as much. There is no house to which one would return, having left it, though it were the hogshead out of which one had moved into a kilderkin; for those associations whose perishing leaves us free, and preserves to us what little youth we have, were otherwise perpetuated to our burden and bondage. Let some one else, who has also escaped from his past, have your old house; he will find it new and untroubled by memories, while you, under another roof, enjoy a present that borders only upon the future.

ABOUT THE AUTHOR

William Dean Howells (March 1, 1837 – May 11, 1920) was an American realist author and literary critic.

Born in Martins Ferry, Ohio, originally Martinsville, to William Cooper and Mary Dean Howells, Howells was the second of eight children. His father was a newspaper editor and printer, and the father moved frequently around Ohio. Howells began to help his father with typesetting and printing work at an early age. In 1852, his father arranged to have one of Howells' poems published in the Ohio State Journal without telling him.

He wrote his first novel, The Wedding Journey, in 1872, but his literary reputation took off with the realist novel, A Modern Instance, published in 1882, which described the decay of a marriage. His 1885 novel The Rise of Silas Lapham is perhaps his best known, describing the rise and fall of an American entrepreneur in the paint business. His social views were also strongly reflected in the novels Annie Kilburn (1888) and A Hazard of New Fortunes (1890). He was particularly outraged by the trials resulting from the Haymarket Riot.

In 1904, he was one of the first seven chosen for membership in the American Academy of Arts and Letters, of which he became president.

Choose from Thousands of 1stWorldLibrary Classics By

A. M. Barnard	Booth Tarkington	Edward Everett Hale
Ada Leverson	Boyd Cable	Edward J. O'Biren
Adolphus William Ward	Bram Stoker	Edward S. Ellis
Aesop	C. Collodi	Edwin L. Arnold
Agatha Christie	C. E. Orr	Eleanor Atkins
Alexander Aaronsohn	C. M. Ingleby	Eleanor Hallowell Abbott
Alexander Kielland	Carolyn Wells	Eliot Gregory
Alexandre Dumas	Catherine Parr Traill	Elizabeth Gaskell
Alfred Gatty	Charles A. Eastman	Elizabeth McCracken
Alfred Ollivant	Charles Amory Beach	Elizabeth Von Arnim
Alice Duer Miller	Charles Dickens	Ellem Key
Alice Turner Curtis	Charles Dudley Warner	Emerson Hough
Alice Dunbar	Charles Farrar Browne	Emilie F. Carlen
Allen Chapman	Charles Ives	Emily Bronte
Alleyne Ireland	Charles Kingsley	Emily Dickinson
Ambrose Bierce	Charles Klein	Enid Bagnold
Amelia E. Barr	Charles Hanson Towne	Enilor Macartney Lane
Amory H. Bradford	Charles Lathrop Pack	Erasmus W. Jones
Andrew Lang	Charles Romyn Dake	Ernie Howard Pie
Andrew McFarland Davis	Charles Whibley	Ethel May Dell
Andy Adams	Charles Willing Beale	Ethel Turner
Angela Brazil	Charlotte M. Braeme	Ethel Watts Mumford
Anna Alice Chapin	Charlotte M. Yonge	Eugene Sue
Anna Sewell	Charlotte Perkins Stetson	Eugenie Foa
Annie Besant	Clair W. Hayes	Eugene Wood
Annie Hamilton Donnell	Clarence Day Jr.	Eustace Hale Ball
Annie Payson Call	Clarence E. Mulford	Evelyn Everett-green
Annie Roe Carr	Clemence Housman	Everard Cotes
Annonaymous	Confucius	F. H. Cheley
Anton Chekhov	Coningsby Dawson	F. J. Cross
Archibald Lee Fletcher	Cornelis DeWitt Wilcox	F. Marion Crawford
Arnold Bennett	Cyril Burleigh	Fannie E. Newberry
Arthur C. Benson	D. H. Lawrence	Federick Austin Ogg
Arthur Conan Doyle	Daniel Defoe	Ferdinand Ossendowski
Arthur M. Winfield	David Garnett	Fergus Hume
Arthur Ransome	Dinah Craik	Florence A. Kilpatrick
Arthur Schnitzler	Don Carlos Janes	Fremont B. Deering
Arthur Train	Donald Keyhoe	Francis Bacon
Atticus	Dorothy Kilner	Francis Darwin
B.H. Baden-Powell	Dougan Clark	Frances Hodgson Burnett
B. M. Bower	Douglas Fairbanks	Frances Parkinson Keyes
B. C. Chatterjee	E. Nesbit	Frank Gee Patchin
Baroness Emmuska Orczy	E. P. Roe	Frank Harris
Baroness Orczy	E. Phillips Oppenheim	Frank Jewett Mather
Basil King	E. S. Brooks	Frank L. Packard
Bayard Taylor	Earl Barnes	Frank V. Webster
Ben Macomber	Edgar Rice Burroughs	Frederic Stewart Isham
Bertha Muzzy Bower	Edith Van Dyne	Frederick Trevor Hill
Bjornstjerne Bjornson	Edith Wharton	Frederick Winslow Taylor

Friedrich Kerst	Hayden Carruth	James Branch Cabell
Friedrich Nietzsche	Helent Hunt Jackson	James DeMille
Fyodor Dostoyevsky	Helen Nicolay	James Joyce
G.A. Henty	Hendrik Conscience	James Lane Allen
G.K. Chesterton	Hendy David Thoreau	James Lane Allen
Gabrielle E. Jackson	Henri Barbusse	James Oliver Curwood
Garrett P. Serviss	Henrik Ibsen	James Oppenheim
Gaston Leroux	Henry Adams	James Otis
George A. Warren	Henry Ford	James R. Driscoll
George Ade	Henry Frost	Jane Abbott
Geroge Bernard Shaw	Henry James	Jane Austen
George Cary Eggleston	Henry Jones Ford	Jane L. Stewart
George Durston	Henry Seton Merriman	Janet Aldridge
George Ebers	Henry W Longfellow	Jens Peter Jacobsen
George Eliot	Herbert A. Giles	Jerome K. Jerome
George Gissing	Herbert Carter	Jessie Graham Flower
George MacDonald	Herbert N. Casson	John Buchan
George Meredith	Herman Hesse	John Burroughs
George Orwell	Hildegard G. Frey	John Cournos
George Sylvester Viereck	Homer	John F. Kennedy
George Tucker	Honore De Balzac	John Gay
George W. Cable	Horace B. Day	John Glasworthy
George Wharton James	Horace Walpole	John Habberton
Gertrude Atherton	Horatio Alger Jr.	John Joy Bell
Gordon Casserly	Howard Pyle	John Kendrick Bangs
Grace E. King	Howard R. Garis	John Milton
Grace Gallatin	Hugh Lofting	John Philip Sousa
Grace Greenwood	Hugh Walpole	John Taintor Foote
Grant Allen	Humphry Ward	Jonas Lauritz Idemil Lie
Guillermo A. Sherwell	Ian Maclaren	Jonathan Swift
Gulielma Zollinger	Inez Haynes Gillmore	Joseph A. Altsheler
Gustav Flaubert	Irving Bacheller	Joseph Carey
H. A. Cody	Isabel Cecilia Williams	Joseph Conrad
H. B. Irving	Isabel Hornibrook	Joseph E. Badger Jr
H.C. Bailey	Israel Abrahams	Joseph Hergesheimer
H. G. Wells	Ivan Turgenev	Joseph Jacobs
H. H. Munro	J.G.Austin	Jules Vernes
H. Irving Hancock	J. Henri Fabre	Julian Hawthrone
H. R. Naylor	J. M. Barrie	Julie A Lippmann
H. Rider Haggard	J. M. Walsh	Justin Huntly McCarthy
H. W. C. Davis	J. Macdonald Oxley	Kakuzo Okakura
Haldeman Julius	J. R. Miller	Karle Wilson Baker
Hall Caine	J. S. Fletcher	Kate Chopin
Hamilton Wright Mabie	J. S. Knowles	Kenneth Grahame
Hans Christian Andersen	J. Storer Clouston	Kenneth McGaffey
Harold Avery	J. W. Duffield	Kate Langley Bosher
Harold McGrath	Jack London	Kate Langley Bosher
Harriet Beecher Stowe	Jacob Abbott	Katherine Cecil Thurston
Harry Castlemon	James Allen	Katherine Stokes
Harry Coghill	James Andrews	L. A. Abbot
Harry Houidini	James Baldwin	L. T. Meade

L. Frank Baum
Latta Griswold
Laura Dent Crane
Laura Lee Hope
Laurence Housman
Lawrence Beasley
Leo Tolstoy
Leonid Andreyev
Lewis Carroll
Lewis Sperry Chafer
Lilian Bell
Lloyd Osbourne
Louis Hughes
Louis Joseph Vance
Louis Tracy
Louisa May Alcott
Lucy Fitch Perkins
Lucy Maud Montgomery
Luther Benson
Lydia Miller Middleton
Lyndon Orr
M. Corvus
M. H. Adams
Margaret E. Sangster
Margret Howth
Margaret Vandercook
Margaret W. Hungerford
Margret Penrose
Maria Edgeworth
Maria Thompson Daviess
Mariano Azuela
Marion Polk Angellotti
Mark Overton
Mark Twain
Mary Austin
Mary Catherine Crowley
Mary Cole
Mary Hastings Bradley
Mary Roberts Rinehart
Mary Rowlandson
M. Wollstonecraft Shelley
Maud Lindsay
Max Beerbohm
Myra Kelly
Nathaniel Hawthrone
Nicolo Machiavelli
O. F. Walton
Oscar Wilde

Owen Johnson
P.G. Wodehouse
Paul and Mabel Thorne
Paul G. Tomlinson
Paul Severing
Percy Brebner
Percy Keese Fitzhugh
Peter B. Kyne
Plato
Quincy Allen
R. Derby Holmes
R. L. Stevenson
R. S. Ball
Rabindranath Tagore
Rahul Alvares
Ralph Bonehill
Ralph Henry Barbour
Ralph Victor
Ralph Waldo Emmerson
Rene Descartes
Ray Cummings
Rex Beach
Rex E. Beach
Richard Harding Davis
Richard Jefferies
Richard Le Gallienne
Robert Barr
Robert Frost
Robert Gordon Anderson
Robert L. Drake
Robert Lansing
Robert Lynd
Robert Michael Ballantyne
Robert W. Chambers
Rosa Nouchette Carey
Rudyard Kipling
Saint Augustine
Samuel B. Allison
Samuel Hopkins Adams
Sarah Bernhardt
Sarah C. Hallowell
Selma Lagerlof
Sherwood Anderson
Sigmund Freud
Standish O'Grady
Stanley Weyman
Stella Benson
Stella M. Francis

Stephen Crane
Stewart Edward White
Stijn Streuvels
Swami Abhedananda
Swami Parmananda
T. S. Ackland
T. S. Arthur
The Princess Der Ling
Thomas A. Janvier
Thomas A Kempis
Thomas Anderton
Thomas Bailey Aldrich
Thomas Bulfinch
Thomas De Quincey
Thomas Dixon
Thomas H. Huxley
Thomas Hardy
Thomas More
Thornton W. Burgess
U. S. Grant
Upton Sinclair
Valentine Williams
Various Authors
Vaughan Kester
Victor Appleton
Victor G. Durham
Victoria Cross
Virginia Woolf
Wadsworth Camp
Walter Camp
Walter Scott
Washington Irving
Wilbur Lawton
Wilkie Collins
Willa Cather
Willard F. Baker
William Dean Howells
William le Queux
W. Makepeace Thackeray
William W. Walter
William Shakespeare
Winston Churchill
Yei Theodora Ozaki
Yogi Ramacharaka
Young E. Allison
Zane Grey

Lightning Source UK Ltd.
Milton Keynes UK
UKOW03n0621161014

240180UK00001B/7/P